MACMILLAN MASTER GUIDES

GENERAL EDITOR: JAMES GI

Published

JANE AUSTEN	*Emma* Norman Page
	Sense and Sensibility Judy Simons
	Persuasion Judy Simons
	Pride and Prejudice Raymond Wilson
	Mansfield Park Richard Wirdnam
SAMUEL BECKETT	*Waiting for Godot* Jennifer Birkett
WILLIAM BLAKE	*Songs of Innocence* and *Songs of Experience* Alan Tomlinson
ROBERT BOLT	*A Man for all Seasons* Leonard Smith
EMILY BRONTË	*Wuthering Heights* Hilda D. Spear
GEOFFREY CHAUCER	*The Miller's Tale* Michael Alexander
	The Pardoner's Tale Geoffrey Lester
	The Wife of Bath's Tale Nicholas Marsh
	The Knight's Tale Anne Samson
	The Prologue to the Canterbury Tales Nigel Thomas and Richard Swan
JOSEPH CONRAD	*The Secret Agent* Andrew Mayne
CHARLES DICKENS	*Bleak House* Dennis Butts
	Great Expectations Dennis Butts
	Hard Times Norman Page
GEORGE ELIOT	*Middlemarch* Graham Handley
	Silas Marner Graham Handley
	The Mill on the Floss Helen Wheeler
HENRY FIELDING	*Joseph Andrews* Trevor Johnson
E. M. FORSTER	*Howards End* Ian Milligan
	A Passage to India Hilda D. Spear
WILLIAM GOLDING	*The Spire* Rosemary Sumner
	Lord of the Flies Raymond Wilson
OLIVER GOLDSMITH	*She Stoops to Conquer* Paul Ranger
THOMAS HARDY	*The Mayor of Casterbridge* Ray Evans
	Tess of the d'Urbervilles James Gibson
	Far from the Madding Crowd Colin Temblett-Wood
JOHN KEATS	*Selected Poems* John Garrett
PHILIP LARKIN	*The Whitsun Weddings* and *The Less Deceived* Andrew Swarbrick
D. H. LAWRENCE	*Sons and Lovers* R. P. Draper
HARPER LEE	*To Kill a Mockingbird* Jean Armstrong
GERARD MANLEY HOPKINS	*Selected Poems* R. J. C. Watt
CHRISTOPHER MARLOWE	*Doctor Faustus* David A. Male
VIRGINIA WOOLF	*To the Lighthouse* John Mepham
THE METAPHYSICAL POETS	Joan van Emden

MACMILLAN MASTER GUIDES

THOMAS MIDDLETON and WILLIAM ROWLEY	*The Changeling* Tony Bromham
ARTHUR MILLER	*The Crucible* Leonard Smith *Death of a Salesman* Peter Spalding
GEORGE ORWELL	*Animal Farm* Jean Armstrong
WILLIAM SHAKESPEARE	*Richard II* Charles Barber *Hamlet* Jean Brooks *King Lear* Francis Casey *Henry V* Peter Davison *The Winter's Tale* Diana Devlin *Julius Caesar* David Elloway *Macbeth* David Elloway *Measure for Measure* Mark Lilly *Henry IV Part I* Helen Morris *Romeo and Juliet* Helen Morris *The Tempest* Kenneth Pickering *A Midsummer Night's Dream* Kenneth Pickering *Coriolanus* Gordon Williams *Antony and Cleopatra* Martin Wine
GEORGE BERNARD SHAW	*St Joan* Leonée Ormond
RICHARD SHERIDAN	*The School for Scandal* Paul Ranger *The Rivals* Jeremy Rowe
ALFRED TENNYSON	*In Memoriam* Richard Gill
ANTHONY TROLLOPE	*Barchester Towers* Ken Newton
JOHN WEBSTER	*The White Devil* and *The Duchess of Malfi* David A. Male

Forthcoming

CHARLOTTE BRONTË	*Jane Eyre* Robert Miles
JOHN BUNYAN	*The Pilgrim's Progress* Beatrice Batson
T. S. ELIOT	*Murder in the Cathedral* Paul Lapworth *Selected Poems* Andrew Swarbrick
BEN JONSON	*Volpone* Michael Stout
RUDYARD KIPLING	*Kim* Leonée Ormond
JOHN MILTON	*Comus* Tom Healy
WILLIAM SHAKESPEARE	*Othello* Tony Bromham *As You Like It* Kiernan Ryan
VIRGINIA WOOLF	*Mrs Dalloway* Julian Pattison
W. B. YEATS	*Selected Poems* Stan Smith

MACMILLAN MASTER GUIDES
SELECTED POEMS OF
GERARD MANLEY HOPKINS

R. J. C. WATT

MACMILLAN
EDUCATION

First edition 1987

Published by
MACMILLAN EDUCATION LTD
Houndmills, Basingstoke, Hampshire RG21 2XS
and London
Companies and representatives
throughout the world

Printed in Hong Kong

British Library Cataloguing in Publication Data
Watt, R. J. C.
Selected poems of Gerard Manley Hopkins.
—(Macmillan master guides)
1. Hopkins, Gerard Manley—Study and
teaching—Outlines, syllabi, etc.
I. Title
821'.8   PR4803.H44Z/
ISBN 0–333–40867–5 Pbk
ISBN 0–333–40868–3 Pbk export

To Margot and Thea

CONTENTS

GENERAL EDITOR'S PREFACE

The aim of the Macmillan Master Guides is to help you to appreciate the book you are studying by providing information about it and by suggesting ways of reading and thinking about it which will lead to a fuller understanding. The section on the writer's life and background has been designed to illustrate those aspects of the writer's life which have influenced the work, and to place it in its personal and literary context. The summaries and critical commentary are of special importance in that each brief summary of the action is followed by an examination of the significant critical points. The space which might have been given to repetitive explanatory notes has been devoted to a detailed analysis of the kind of passage which might confront you in an examination. Literary criticism is concerned with both the broader aspects of the work being studied and with its detail. The ideas which meet us in reading a great work of literature, and their relevance to us today, are an essential part of our study, and our Guides look at the thought of their subject in some detail. But just as essential is the craft with which the writer has constructed his work of art, and this may be considered under several technical headings – characterisation, language, style and stagecraft, for example.

The authors of these Guides are all teachers and writers of wide experience, and they have chosen to write about books they admire and know well in the belief that they can communicate their admiration to you. But you yourself must read and know intimately the book you are studying. No one can do that for you. You should see this book as a lamp-post. Use it to shed light, not to lean against. If you know your text and know what it is saying about life, and how it says it, then you will enjoy it, and there is no better way of passing an examination in literature.

JAMES GIBSON

ACKNOWLEDGEMENTS

I owe thanks to the Revd Paul Edwards S. J., until recently Master of Campion Hall, Oxford, who kindly allowed me to use the Hopkins manuscripts there, and to the late Frank Pickstock for first giving me the opportunity to teach Hopkins. Alan Tomlinson's patience with my abrupt interruptions, and intelligent answers to my questions, have been much appreciated. To Stan Smith go special thanks for tireless entrepreneurship, encouragement and criticism. I am much indebted, consciously and unconsciously, to previous writers on Hopkins, too many to number. I should like to express my gratitude here.

R. J. C. WATT

The Elm Tree, Perthshire by J. McIntosh Patrick. Photograph reproduced by kind permission of J. McIntosh Patrick.

1 GERARD MANLEY HOPKINS

1.1 INTRODUCTION

Gerard Manley Hopkins completed fewer than fifty mature English poems – that is, excluding fragments, juvenilia, and poems written in other languages. And of these completed poems, the vast majority, nearly forty, are no longer than sonnets. It seems a fairly small body of work when compared to the poetic copiousness of some of the other great Victorians. These few poems were all written with the single aim of promoting the greater glory of God. An unsympathetic reader might feel that Hopkins had a limited poetic range (though one might reply that in choosing to write of God, man, and the world Hopkins chose subjects almost inconceivably vast).

What is more, many of his poems are crammed with tortuous difficulties of expression and with stylistic devices which on first acquaintance may appear odd, even mannered. Some of the techniques they use are so radically experimental that when explained they still provoke amazement among intelligent readers with a wide knowledge of poetry. And to cap it all, nearly every one of Hopkins's poems gives embodiment to an intense and demanding religious vision, the theology of a wholly dedicated Jesuit priest who never permitted himself to express a single thought which was at odds with his religious faith and vocation.

Put like this, it might sound like a recipe for poetic disaster. We might expect to find Hopkins in a dusty footnote amid the curiosities of literary history. Yet in reality few people would now deny that Hopkins is among the greatest of nineteenth-century poets. And some readers, who value poetry because it is there that language itself is at its most powerful and most highly organised, would set Hopkins even higher, arguing that after reading him every other poet in English seems slack or dilute.

Hopkins is a surprising and exciting poet. Much of his work makes big demands on the reader at a first encounter. But once that price of overcoming initial difficulty has been paid, the rewards are great. Complicated though his poems often are, Hopkins nevertheless believed that poems should make literal and graspable sense. They should have, he wrote, one of two kinds of clearness: 'either the meaning to be felt without effort as fast as one reads or else, if dark at first reading, when once made out *to explode*'. He himself wrote poems of both kinds. Other people's poems which were *merely* difficult, without any compensating reward, he called 'totally unexplosive'.

This book aims to provide some aids to combustion. It is a guide to those aspects of the poetry which may be 'dark at first reading'. A brief account of his life is followed by short sections on topics such as sprung rhythm, inscape, and Duns Scotus which are essential to the understanding of many of the poems. The main part of the book discusses the poems themselves and offers ways of approaching their meanings. Beyond that, his intricate poetic effects generate an inexhaustible richness of suggestion which could not be covered in adequate detail in any single book, let alone one of this length. This book, then, cannot be read without close and constant reference to the poems themselves. It is an invitation to think for oneself about each poem, line by line and effect by effect, in the detail which it deserves. For only in the mind of each reader can there take place the work which is necessary if the meaning of the poem is 'to explode'.

1.2 LIFE

Childhood

Gerard Manley Hopkins came from a cultivated and comfortably prosperous middle-class Victorian family. Born at Stratford, Essex on 28 July 1844, he was the eldest of nine children, one of whom died in infancy. His father, Manley Hopkins, ran a marine insurance company in the City of London; earlier generations of his father's family had been Essex fishermen. His mother was the daughter of a London doctor who had been a fellow student of Keats.

When Hopkins was eight the family moved to a house called Oak Hill in Hampstead, then a pleasantly rustic suburb on the edge of North London. Hopkins went to school in nearby Highgate, where he distinguished himself in Classics and also began to write poetry. Despite his brilliance as a pupil, Hopkins later wrote: 'I had no love for my schooldays and wished to banish the remembrance of them'. Though uninterested in school games, he was a fearless climber of trees, and in other ways his strength – of will, if not of body – was extraordinary. He once abstained from liquids for days on end in order to win a small bet. He was capable of rash courage, as he showed when he quarrelled with his dictatorial headmaster: 'Dyne and I had a terrific altercation. I was driven out of patience and cheeked him wildly, and he blazed into me with his riding-whip.'

Artistic, musical, and linguistic accomplishments were widespread in the family. An aunt taught Hopkins drawing and music. His father wrote and published verse. Two of his brothers were eventually to gain reputations as artists, but otherwise the family's talents remained those of gifted amateurs, never sufficiently tested by need or crisis to rise to artistic greatness. With Gerard Manley Hopkins it was to be otherwise.

At twelve years old he wrote that a school friend was 'a kaleido-scopic, parti-coloured, harlequinesque, thaumatropic being'. Though the thaumatrope (a card with different pictures on each side, so that when spun rapidly the pictures seem to merge) was a familiar enough Victorian toy and the word therefore less unfamiliar than it now appears, the delighted command of language shown here is still remarkable for a twelve-year-old, and foreshadows much to come.

His talents at poetry and drawing were already evident during his schooldays. They are the work of a young man, showing remarkable ability but only the occasional hint of his later originality. His early poems are largely imitations of Keats – who had lived nearby – and the drawings, with their meticulous eye for natural detail, are in the manner advocated by John Ruskin, the most influential of Victorian art critics.

University

Hopkins won a scholarship at Balliol College, Oxford, and entered the university in 1863. The next four years were to be crucial in shaping his destiny. By the 1860s Oxford was a place of rising academic standards, strenuous morality, and intense spirituality. As one of the ablest undergraduates at the most intellectually distinguished college, Hopkins found himself the subject of high expectations. Striving was already part of his nature. His university studies were in Greek and Latin language and literature, philosophy, and history. He became known as 'the star of Balliol', and the future career he may then have imagined for himself is hinted at in an essay he wrote where he illustrates a logical chain of development as follows: 'Scholarship University First Class Honours Fellowship Orders Bishopric'.

If his academic work was important to him, so was the company of friends. 'I have not breakfasted in my own rooms for 10 days I think', he wrote, giving us a glimpse of his sociable nature. Though always given to strict examination of his conscience and behaviour, Hopkins was no prig or killjoy, and in one letter cheerfully records how he and some friends celebrated the end of an examination by 'proceed[ing] to booze at the Mitre . . . I forgot to pay my share'. Some of his undergraduate friendships were to last throughout his life, and the loss of others is a theme which recurs in his poetry.

But his other preoccupation, in common with nearly all his contemporaries, was religion. The climate of religious intensity which existed in Oxford in the mid-nineteenth century was unlike anything in the ordinary experience of most Westerners alive today. To arrive at that University in the 1860s was, religiously speaking, to find oneself in the middle of a pitched battle. Nor was it some parochial squabble, for the whole Anglican church was being re-shaped by the clash which was focused in Oxford between Tractarianism and the Broad Church movement. Tractarianism, which took its name from a series of publications called *Tracts for the Times*, had begun in Oxford in 1833 and in the following thirty years the conflicts which it engendered transformed religious debate. The Tractarians brought to religion a new sense of its high spiritual purpose, regenerated its moral authority, and did much to establish the religious earnestness which we think of as characteristically mid-Victorian. It was in this High Anglican faith that Hopkins had grown up.

Tractarianism set a high value on church ritual, and consequently had always been suspected by its enemies of being too close to Roman Catholicism. And Catholicism, at one time and another ever since the Reformation, had been accused of being an enemy within the state because its adherents were obliged to owe allegiance to the Pope as well as to the British monarch. Such controversies, then, had political as well as religious implications. The suspicion that the Tractarians were too close to Rome was given plausibility when John Henry Newman, one of the founders of the Tractarian movement, himself became a convert to the Catholic faith in 1845 – the most famous conversion of the century.

But by the 1860s when Hopkins became an undergraduate the Tractarians were under threat not only from Roman Catholicism but also from something even newer, the Broad Church movement. Its leader was Benjamin Jowett, of Hopkins's own college, Balliol. The arch-exponent of Plato, Jowett adopted the Socratic method of questioning and debate as his weapon in the pursuit of truth. Nothing was to be taken for granted; all assumptions were to be tested in the light of evidence and logic. Jowett was bold enough to challenge the divinity of Christ and the literal truth of the Bible. Such an assault upon traditional religious faith had already been gathering strength for several decades, aided by the discoveries of geology, the theory of evolution, and exact Biblical scholarship. To many it seemed that the very foundations of religion were under attack. Man's sense of himself, his purpose and place in the world, and the organisation of his society – all of which were traditionally supported by religion – were therefore open to question too.

Hopkins the Tractarian found himself caught between the opposing forces of Broad Church on one side and Roman Catholicism on the other. Great charm, great intellectual force, and great bitterness were shown by all parties in the struggle. He was as near to the eye of the storm as it was possible for anyone to be. For Liddon and Pusey, leaders of the Tractarians, were his confessors. And Jowett, leader of the Broad Church party, was one of his tutors. It was an impossible position. As he wrote to Newman, 'All our minds you see were ready to go at a touch'. In 1866, during his last year at Oxford, Hopkins took the irrevocable decision of his life and was received into the Catholic church by Newman himself.

Hopkins's poems and journals contain few hints about the exact process which led him to conversion. There is no need to speculate overmuch, though: his High Church starting-point, with its emphasis on ritual, was not so far from Rome in some matters of church practice, though the step across was still a major one, certain to cause distress to family and teachers. And above all there was his temperament, one which craved certainty and discipline and which rejected compromises. There are hints that his sense of the sordidness and triviality of the ordinary things of the world helped lead him to the position where he would finally renounce a worldly life. Love was central to his vision of Christ, and the Catholic doctrine of the real presence of Christ in the Eucharist was full of meaning for him.

Life as a Jesuit

Hopkins was too uncompromising a man to do anything by halves. Having decided to act upon his new convictions and join the Catholic church, he was not content to remain a lay Catholic. Almost at once he decided to devote his life to the priesthood. He chose the Jesuits, the most militant, disciplined, and rigorous of Catholic orders. In 1868 he began a course of training for priesthood which was to last nine years, and at the same time burnt some copies of his poems in the belief that the writing of poetry was a self-indulgence for one who had decided to dedicate his life to God. It was his own decision, not a rule of his order: he recorded that he 'resolved to write no more, as not belonging to my profession, unless it were by the wish of my superiors'. For the next seven years he wrote no poetry. His imaginative energies were poured instead into his journals and letters, when he had time to spare for them. They show that he was happy in the service of God.

His training for the priesthood was long and thorough. He spent two years as a novice at Manresa House in Roehampton, London, then three years studying philosophy at Stonyhurst College in Lancashire. He returned to Roehampton to teach Rhetoric for a year, and then in 1874 began three years' study of theology at St Beuno's College near Tremeirchion in the beautiful Vale of Clwyd in

North Wales. It was there in 1875 that a tactful hint from one of his superiors convinced him that he might resume the writing of poetry without detracting from his vocation. He needed no further prompting, and at once his mature style, vastly different from that of his early poetry, burst forth. 1876 saw him working on 'The Wreck of the Deutschland', his greatest single poem, and the following year produced at least ten of his finest sonnets.

After he resumed writing in 1875 all Hopkins's poetry was intimately bound up with his religious beliefs and vocation. It is important to realise that there was no conflict between Hopkins the priest and Hopkins the poet, and it is meaningless to wonder what kind of poetry he might have written had he not been a Jesuit. The poetry as we have it draws its strength from his religious vision.

The work of a priest

From the time of his ordination as a priest in 1877 Hopkins had fewer than twelve years left to live. The next seven were spent as any Jesuit might expect, engaged in parish work and preaching, being moved around the country at short notice as and when a need arose. Brief periods at Chesterfield and London were followed by a return to Oxford for his first assignment of any length. It was not a complete success: he was denied the chance of exercising his ministry among the undergraduates, and among his middle-class parishioners he seems to have found more sophistication than religious devotion. He apparently longed for a bigger challenge, which lay among the poor of the North. Yet this was one of the more fruitful periods for his poetry: the year in Oxford produced, among other poems, 'Binsey Poplars', 'Duns Scotus's Oxford', 'Henry Purcell', 'The Candle Indoors', 'Andromeda', and 'Peace'.

There followed three happy months at Bedford Leigh, a small industrial town near Manchester. As one scholar puts it, 'In this smoke-sodden little town he came up against people who needed him desperately, and their need was what he needed'. But the bigger challenge was to come next. From 1880 to 1882 he came into the closest contact with the misery and squalor of the great industrial cities. Daily he found himself struggling against urban poverty and drunkenness on a gigantic scale. The experience gave him very pronounced views about so-called British 'civilisation': 'My Liverpool and Glasgow experience laid upon my mind a conviction, a truly crushing conviction, of . . . the misery of the poor in general, of the degradation even of our race, of the hollowness of this century's civilisation'.

Hopkins was an intelligent man who used his eyes, and such experiences were not a new discovery but a reminder of what he had known for years. As early as 1871 he had written 'it is a dreadful thing for the greatest and most necessary part of a very rich nation to live a hard life without dignity, knowledge, comforts, delight, or hopes in the midst of plenty – which plenty they make. They profess that they do not care what they wreck and burn, the old order and civilisation must be destroyed. This is a dreadful look out but what has the old civilisation done for them? As it at present stands in England it is itself in great measure founded on wrecking. But they got none of the spoils, they came in for nothing but harm from it then and thereafter. England has grown hugely wealthy but this wealth has not reached the working classes; I expect it has made their condition worse.'

He never altered these views: shortly before his death he wrote 'Our whole civilisation is dirty, yea filthy, and especially in the north; for is it not dirty, yea filthy, to pollute the air as Blackburn and Widnes and St. Helen's are polluted and the water as the Thames and the Clyde and the Irwell are polluted?'

Hopkins's work in the industrial cities, it seems, finally broke his health, which had always been precarious. Within months of starting work in Liverpool he said he was 'so fagged, so harried and gallied up and down'. Thereafter he was 'always tired, always jaded'.

A retreat from the world

The three years after leaving Glasgow in 1881 were spent on familiar ground, first in a return to Roehampton for his Tertianship, a year of 'second noviceship', meditation and spiritual renewal, prescribed for all Jesuits as a prelude to their final vows. This seclusion was a complete contrast to the years of intense pastoral work: at such times, as he put it, 'We see no newspapers nor read any but spiritual books'. The chance to devote himself wholly and directly to God was welcome: 'my mind is here more at peace than it has ever been and I would gladly live all my life, if it were so to be, in as great or a greater seclusion from the world and be busied only with God'.

Last years

An eighteen-month return to Stonyhurst to teach Classics was followed in 1884 by his final appointment, Professor of Greek at University College, Dublin. No doubt his superiors had decided that scholarly work and teaching would be most congenial to him. It was not to be: in poor health, and cut off from his family and country, he was often in dejection. Examination work in enormous quantities was another dispiriting burden: 'I have 557 papers on hand: let those who have been thro' the like say what that means'. 'It is killing work to examine a nation.'

By 1885 he was writing of 'that coffin of weakness and dejection in which I live'. The melancholy to which, he said, he had all his life been subject became more constant. One form it took was a 'daily anxiety about work to be done, which makes me break off or never finish all that lies outside that work . . . when I am at the worst, though my judgment is never affected, my state is much like madness'.

His strong interest in politics was another source of gloom. He was disturbed by the Irish Home Rule movement and by the involvement of his church, the Society of Jesus, and his university colleagues in advancing it: 'a partly unlawful cause, promoted by partly unlawful means', he called it. That repeated word 'partly' is revealing: it shows the hesitation of a man who was now caught by a contradiction. All his life he had been an ardent English patriot, but now he was forced to recognise that there was at least some justice in the Irish cause, and hence in the point of view which saw England as a brutal exploiter and oppressor.

'I have never wavered in my vocation, but I have not lived up to it', Hopkins once wrote. When the standard aimed at is that of perfection, the ideally Christian life, then not to live up to it is unavoidable. Most Christians accept that, but Hopkins felt it keenly as a failure. Many who knew him judged otherwise. The poet Coventry Patmore called him a 'saintly' man, ' a Catholic of the most scrupulous strictness' but one whose 'religion had absolutely no narrowing effect upon his general opinions and sympathies'. 'There was something in all his words and manners which were at once a rebuke and an attraction to all who could only aspire to be like him.'

In the Sonnets of Desolation and other poems from his years in Ireland he cried out against his lot. But there is all the difference in the world between crying to God for mercy and doubting God's love or power. Nowhere is there the slightest evidence that Hopkins's faith was ever damaged or lessened. 'I have never wavered in my vocation'. Though simply put, it is a claim which a less humble man might well have been proud of. Scrupulously, even self-punishingly honest, Hopkins meant what he said, always.

Late in life, though he was still writing great poems, he often felt that his creative faculties had deserted him and that he had failed to complete any other work of lasting significance. At such moments he could console himself with the belief that such things were not what God would judge him by: as he put it, 'if we care for fine verses how much more for a noble life!' In one letter he summed up his sense of barrenness in this forceful image: 'Nothing comes: I am a eunuch'. Yet he added, significantly, 'but it is for the kingdom of heaven's sake'.

Hopkins died in Dublin of typhoid fever in June 1889 at the age of 45. His last words, when he knew very well that death was at hand, were 'I am so happy'.

2 AN APPROACH TO
THE POETRY

This chapter provides a guide to some of the difficulties which new readers may encounter in studying Hopkins, beginning with his often innovative uses of poetic form and technique, and then discussing some of the ideas which recur throughout his poetry.

2.1 THE SONNET

Hopkins preferred the sonnet form to all others. Though we may think of the Elizabethan or the Romantic periods as the high points in the history of the sonnet in English, the sonnet was also highly fashionable among poets both good and bad in Hopkins's lifetime. His reasons for being attracted to it, however, went beyond fashion. As a complex and elaborate verse form, it offers difficulties and constraints, and enforces artistic discipline, in a way that appealed to his temperament.

The two forms of the sonnet in our language are known as the Italian sonnet, which Hopkins always preferred, the first eight lines Shakespearean). Both consist of fourteen lines of iambic pentameter; the difference between them is in their rhyme-schemes. The Italian sonnet rhymes *abbaabbacdcdcd* (though variations are permitted in the last six rhymes), whereas the English sonnet rhymes *ababcdcde-fefgg*. Some important consequences stem from this difference. In the Italian sonnet which Hopkins always preferred, the first eight lines (the *octave*) and the remaining six (the *sestet*) become two distinct units, because up to line eight we hear only two rhyming sounds, the *a* and the *b*, and after line eight those two never recur. Hence the break between lines eight and nine becomes the major turning-point (called the 'turn' or the 'volta') in the Italian sonnet. Such a sonnet 'begins' twice, first at line one and again at line nine. The English sonnet's rhyme-scheme, by contrast, tends to divide the poem into three quatrains (groups of four lines) and a concluding couplet.

Poets who choose the Italian form can exploit this feature by making the sestet mark a change of pace or mood, or introduce a new turn in the thought. In the sonnets which Hopkins wrote in Wales, for example, the octave usually deals with the physical world and the sestet with the spiritual or metaphysical implications of what he observes.

The other striking feature of the Italian sonnet, when written in English, is also probably the reason why Hopkins inclined to it: it is harder to write. Compared to languages such as Italian, the English language is relatively short of rhyming words. (This is because Italian is an inflected language and so similar word-endings can be 'manufactured', while word-order is not so important to meaning as it is in English.) In writing a sonnet of the Italian form the poet has to find four *a* rhymes and four *b* rhymes, a far harder challenge than the English sonnet, which demands nothing more than pairs of rhyming words.

Eventually he came to feel that even these resources were insufficient, and that the conventional sonnet was too brief and not weighty enough for really ambitious poetry. His first radical innovation was to apply to the sonnet his metrical innovation called sprung rhythm (see below), which he had already perfected in 'The Wreck of the Deutschland'. This gave the possibility of much longer and weightier lines. He began this re-shaping in the sonnets of 1877 written in Wales. Sometimes too he altered the actual number of lines. 'Tom's Garland' and 'That Nature is a Heraclitean Fire' are 'caudated' sonnets, that is, having a coda or 'tail'. Such developments reached their extremes in some of his later poems, and are discussed in the chapter of this book called 'The Sonnet Surpassed'. 'Pied Beauty' and 'Peace', on the other hand, are 'curtal' sonnets, shortened or curtailed in length while preserving the proportions of the original.

2.2 SOME TECHNICAL RESOURCES

The significance of the rhyme-scheme in an Italian sonnet has already been mentioned. In many poets, rhyme is a less powerful resource for the creation of meaning than rhythm and metre. But in Hopkins, rhyme and certain related devices are often of great importance. Hopkins liked rhyme as a way of binding the language of his poems more tightly together. He also attached special importance to it because he thought that something very like it was one of the principles by which the world itself was organised. For although no two created things are *exactly* alike, each particular thing in the world has *some* features in common with other particular things. This same principle of simultaneous likeness and unlikeness is, of course, to be found in any pair of rhyming words. As Hopkins once put it, 'all beauty may by a metaphor be called rhyme'.

For these reasons Hopkins loved not only rhyme but certain related devices which bind words together: *assonance* (the correspondence of vowel sounds between words or syllables) and *alliteration* (the correspondence of consonantal sounds between words or syllables). Hopkins tends to use such devices not on their own but in rich combination. Take the evocation of church-bells in 'As kingfishers catch fire': 'each hung bell's/ Bow swung finds tongue to fling out broad its name'. This goes beyond assonance to *internal rhyme*, for 'hung, 'swung' and 'tongue' are full rhymes although none is in the conventional rhyming position at the line-end. In this same example *onomatopoeia* (where the sound of the word echoes the sense) is also at work: we seem to hear a dominant note, as of one deep bell, in the repeated *ung* sounds, followed by a peal of higher notes in the vowels and diphthongs of 'fling out broad its name'. And alliteration, of the consonants *b* and *f*, also contributes to the effect.

Hopkins's liking for the careful organisation of sound reached its height in a device which he found in Welsh poetry and adopted for his own. Called by its Welsh name *cynghanedd* (we might call it consonant-chime), it is a systematic use of alliteration and internal rhyme in complex patterns governed by strict rules. There are several varieties of cynghanedd: for more detailed information see the books by Norman MacKenzie and W. H. Gardner listed in the section on further reading. A good example is the line

> The down-dugged ground-hugged grey

Here we have internal rhyme ('dugged' and 'hugged'), and assonance ('down' and 'ground'). But the real skill is in the patterning of the consonants. Those which are underlined above reveal a pattern of sounds (n-d-gg-d-gr) which is repeated, so that the second part of the line is an echo of the first. Two more examples, chosen from among many, are

> To bathe in his fall-gold mercies, to breathe in his all-
>   fire glances.

And

> Left hand, off land, I hear the lark ascend

Hopkins wrote of 'the endless labour of recasting' such lines as these to achieve the patterning of sounds he wanted. His word for the effect was 'chimes', which suggests why he thought it worth pursuing: not merely for decoration but to reflect the intricate and harmonious interrelationship of things in the created world.

Hopkins's *diction* (choice of words) gives his poetry a highly distinctive air. Often it provides verbal equivalents for his precise observations of the visual world. In 'Inversnaid' the rowan tree is called 'beadbonny', a word which focuses attention on the tree's most striking visual feature, its clusters of red berries in autumn. Or in 'Binsey Poplars' the trees, we are told, 'dandled a sandalled/ Shadow'. The dancing pattern of light and shade coming through the foliage is evoked by the connotations of that unusual adjective 'sandalled', suggesting silent movement and interlaced design. Or in 'Harry Ploughman' the 'rope-over' thigh creates a far sharper visual image of taut, tense limbs than ordinary adjectives such as 'muscular' or 'sinewy' could do.

Other effects depend on a literal, semi-primitive diction. Man's spirit, he says in 'The Sea and the Skylark', dwells in his 'bone-house': the suggestion there of a skeletal prison which confines the soul is far more effective than the more ordinary synonym 'body' could evoke. Here he is using a technique borrowed from Anglo-Saxon poetry to give an idea visual immediacy by the use of a metaphor made from compounded nouns. A famous example from Anglo-Saxon verse is the use of the term 'whale-road' for the sea. More generally, Hopkins's style often makes effective use of plain, short, forceful words of Anglo-Saxon origin.

Yet he did not eschew that alternative resource of the English language, the words of Latin or Greek origin with their resonance and speed. For instance, in the lines 'Be adored among men,/ God, three-numberèd form', try replacing 'adored' with 'loved' and 'numberèd' (pronounced as three syllables) with 'named' and see what is lost. Many such words are polysyllabic. For example, in the line 'Generations have trod, have trod, have trod' it is the sheer length of the noun which brings home its suggestion of an interminable process (reinforced of course by the weary repetitive rhythms of the following monosyllabic verbs).

Other notable features of Hopkins's diction include the use of *coinages* (so, for example, the assault of an angry sea is caught in the phrase 'the rash smart *sloggering* brine'); *compound nouns*: (as in 'rockfire' for sparks made by nailed boots); *verbs turned into nouns* ('the *achieve* of, the mastery of the thing!'); and a device learned from his youthful admiration for Keats's poetry, the *compound epithet*, such as those used to describe the city in 'Duns Scotus's Oxford': 'Cuckoo-echoing, bell-swarmèd, lark-charmèd, rook-racked, river-rounded'.

But perhaps the most challenging aspect of Hopkins's style is his unusual *syntax* (grammatical construction, or the way in which words are ordered and related to each other). One simple syntactical device is the inversion of normal word-order, as when in the poem 'Thou art indeed just, Lord' he writes 'why must/ Disappointment all I endeavour end?' Notice how a more normal order – 'disappointment end all I endeavour' – would lose the heavy stress on 'all' and the clever placing of 'end' at the end of the line. This reminds us that effects of syntax, metre, diction, and so on do not exist in isolation but in interplay with each other.

Not all such effects, however, depend upon elaborate or unusual syntax: to begin a poem with the words 'Felix Randal the farrier, O is he dead then?' is to use the word-order of conversation to help catch the accents of a speaking voice surprised by sudden news. In many another poem the frequent exclamations, as well as the syntax, likewise achieve the energy of living *speech*.

Another feature of Hopkins's style is his tendency to omit the unnecessary word to achieve the greatest possible pressure and density of meaning, as when he writes in 'Duns Scotus's Oxford' of 'a base and brickish skirt there, sours/ That neighbour-nature thy grey beauty is grounded/Best in'. There the relative pronoun 'which' has been omitted twice, before 'sours'/ and again after neighbour-nature'. Density of meaning is even greater in a line such as that which ends 'The Wreck of the Deutschland':

> Our hearts' charity's hearth's fire, our thoughts'
> chivalry's thong's Lord.

We might unpack the sense here as 'the fire of the hearth of the charity of our hearts, Lord of the throng of the chivalry of our thoughts'. Hopkins's version, however, achieves more than just extreme conciseness. As the critic Elisabeth Schneider has put it, the line is 'locked together in the hook-and-eye grip of the possessive case'. We may think of the possessive case as being the closest of grammatical relationships. Thus by multiplying the use of the possessive beyond normal expectations Hopkins forces us to ponder what for him was the closest of *actual* relationships, between God and man. Notice how the words 'Our . . . Lord' frame the line, and inside the frame, locked into it by the grammar, are things of the human world. So a line which at first may appear awkward or eccentric turns out to reveal the way that God is inextricably involved in human affairs. Rather than merely asserting or describing the closeness of that relationship, the line *enacts* it, forcing us to experience its intricacy for ourselves as we work to grasp the meaning.

This is language at its most challenging. Each effect is new and unique to its context, and must be studied there.

2.3 SPRUNG RHYTHM

For Hopkins, as for Yeats and many other great poets, poetry was passionate *speech*. It should be as free as living speech is to draw upon all the resources of the language so as to create the maximum amount of powerful meaning. For rhythm and metre, in good poetry, are not mere embellishment but ways of generating meanings, often very precise meanings. 'Why do I employ sprung rhythm at all?' Hopkins wrote. 'Because it is the nearest to the rhythm of prose, that is the native and natural rhythm of speech.'

Now, in conventional English poetic rhythm and metre Hopkins saw one great tyranny. If a poet writes a stressed syllable, he is obliged (irregularities apart) to follow it with its opposite, an unstressed syllable. If he writes an unstressed syllable, he must follow it with a stressed. And so on throughout each line. This applies whether a poem is in iambic verse (where the unstressed syllable is followed by the stressed, as in the word 'employ') or in trochaic, its opposite (as in the word 'follow'). For each metrical unit or 'foot', whether iambic or trochaic, is followed by another of the same kind, setting up an endlessly running pattern of rhythm which alternates between stress and unstress. Hence Hopkins called this conventional scheme 'alternating' or 'running' rhythm.

There are, of course, other metrical possibilities in standard English verse besides the iamb and the trochee: there are, for instance, the feet of three syllables such as the anapaest and the dactyl. But consider Robert Browning's lines:

> I sprang to the stirrup, and Joris, and he;
> I galloped, Dirck galloped, we galloped all three

The effect of repetitive alternation (done deliberately here, of course) is even more marked. Hopkins's point about 'alternating' rhythm still applies.

Hopkins rightly saw that real speech is not at all like alternating rhythm. If in speaking we want to create great emphasis by putting several hard stresses next to each other, we can do so. If, on the other hand, we want to gabble out half a dozen rapid syllables with hardly a stress amongst them, we can again do it in speech. Why not in poetry? Only because of the rule which obliges us, in conventional prosody, to follow a stressed with an unstressed syllable or vice versa. Hopkins therefore abolished this rule, and in doing so arrived at sprung rhythm.

In conventional verse the number of stresses per line is fixed and so is the total number of syllables. A line of iambic pentameter, to take the most common metre in English, thus has five stresses and ten syllables, as in Shakespeare's

Y̆ou bló̆cks, y̆ou stó̆nes, y̆ou wó̆rse thă̆n sé̆nselĕss thí̆ngs

Hopkins saw that in trying to avoid the drawbacks of 'alternating' rhythm it would not do simply to permit total freedom about the number of stresses in a line. For it is the number of stresses, rather than the actual length of a line, which gives a line its weight and makes one line *seem* the same length as another. If successive lines of a poem were to be given very different numbers of *stresses*, chosen at random, the lines would appear to have nothing in common, and would cease to be recognisable as verse at all. But he saw that it would be possible to vary the number of *syllables* in a line almost at will, while retaining a fixed number of stresses, and that this would give him the freedom he wanted: the freedom to put stresses hard up against each other, or widely separated, according to the needs of the meaning.

The essence of sprung rhythm, then, is this. Whereas a line of ordinary verse has a fixed number of stresses *and* a fixed number of syllables, a line in sprung rhythm has only a fixed number of stresses: the number of syllables can vary widely. That is the technical definition, and put that way it may seem confusing or strange. In fact it is perfectly familiar to us all in practice, for it is already widespread in our language. Hopkins acknowledged this: 'I do not say the idea is altogether new; there are hints of it in music, in nursery rhymes and popular jingles, in the poets themselves'. Let us look at one example Hopkins himself gave when first trying to explain sprung rhythm in letters to his baffled friends. Nursery rhymes, he pointed out, are full of it:

Dĭng doṇg bell	(3 stresses, 3 syllables)
Pussy̆'s in thĕ well	(3 stresses, 5 syllables)
Who put hĕr in?	(3 stresses, 4 syllables)
Little Johnny̆ Thin.	(3 stresses, 5 syllables)

The number of stresses is the same in each line, but the number of syllables varies. Of course there is a fixed *minimum* number of syllables, in this case three (see line 1) for otherwise there would be not enough syllables for the stresses to fall on. But the *maximum* number of syllables is unrestricted, and can be surprisingly large. Consider a few lines from another children's rhyme:

Three blind mice	(3 stresses, 3 syllables)
See how they run	(3 stresses, 4 syllables)
They all ran after the farmer's wife	
	(3 stresses, 9 syllables)
Who cut off their tails with a carving knife	
	(3 stresses, 10 syllables)

Because the lines have the same number of *stresses* they seem, subjectively, to be roughly equivalent in 'weight' even though they differ greatly in length. These long lines are achieved by filling out the line with *unstressed* syllables. It may be helpful to think of sprung rhythm in this way: in a sprung line, the number of stresses remains constant, but there can be as few, or as many, *unstressed syllables* as one wishes.

But of course Hopkins was aiming at artistic effects more powerful than those of a nursery rhyme. 'The Wreck of the Deutschland', the first great poem of Hopkins's maturity, was also the first in which he used sprung rhythm, and we may find there some good examples of what he was aiming at. The second stanza of the poem begins:

> I did say yes
> O at lightning and lashed rod

The two hard stresses next to each other on 'lashed rod' have just the whip-like effect needed to emphasise the meaning of the words. As Hopkins explained, in conventional verse he would be compelled to weaken this effect and write something like 'lashed birch-rod' (where the syllable 'birch' is less heavily stressed), simply to comply with the demands of alternating rhythm. Often in his poems he makes use of this power of sprung rhythm to crowd stresses next to each other without any intervening unstressed syllables to dilute the effect. Still in stanza two of 'The Wreck of the Deutschland', we find

> The swoon of a heart that the sweep and the hurl of thee trod
> Hard down with a horror of height

There, the rapid swinging or loping movement of the first line is brought up short by the hammer-blows of 'trod/ Hard down'. This example also illustrates another advantage of sprung rhythm, which is that it easily permits rhythmic effects to be carried on across the break at the end of a line. In fact Hopkins intended poems in sprung rhythm to be scanned continuously from start to finish rather than a line at a time. This running-on of the scansion he called 'overreaving'.

The last two examples show sprung rhythm at its purest. The word 'sprung', as Hopkins wrote, 'means something like *abrupt* and applies by rights only where one stress follows another running, without syllable between'. But he also takes advantage of sprung rhythm at its other extreme, where the stresses are widely separated by unstressed syllables crowding into the line. As always in English poetry, a preponderance of unstressed syllables gives a line rapidity and lightness of movement, because the voice does not have to dwell on what is not heavily stressed. Having given himself the freedom to write almost as many uninterrupted unstresses as he wishes, Hopkins can achieve that lightness of touch as never before in English:

> ，lóvely-felícitous Providence
> Finger of a ténder of, O of a féathery delicacy, the
> bréast of the ，
> Máiden could obey so . . .　　　　　(stanza 31)

There could hardly be a greater contrast between this and a heavily emphatic line such as

> The sóur scythe crínge, and the bléar sháre cóme.
> 　　　　　　　　　　　(stanza 11)

After 'The Wreck of the Deutschland' Hopkins contined to develop his ideas on sprung rhythm. He experimented with some complications such as 'hangers' or 'outrides', unstressed syllables which appear to 'hang' below the line and are not counted in the scanning. And he often toyed with a complicated system of metrical markings which, he hoped, would clarify the way he wanted a line to be performed, though it would scarcely have enhanced the attractiveness of the poems on the page. But he was feeling his way forwards, and his remarks on these extensions to the principles of sprung rhythm are not entirely consistent. The occasional markings of unusual stresses which have found their way into modern editions of his poetry may be disconcerting to the reader at first, but they often help to bring out emphasis and hence meaning.

But even as he was refining upon sprung rhythm he was also, to a limited extent, turning away from it. Many of his later poems are written in sprung rhythm, but a number of others are not. The poems written at the very end of his life abandon it almost entirely, though by that stage Hopkins had learnt to make conventional metre capable of some of the effects of sprung rhythm. Although he had a powerful theoretical turn of mind, he was not a slave to poetic rules: sprung rhythm itself was invented because of the restricting effects of conventional prosodic rules, and it seems that he was not prepared to allow it to become a new tyranny. Instead, in his later work, he uses or lays aside sprung rhythm at will, according to what will best suit the poem in hand.

It is the essence of sprung rhythm which matters more than the details. Its best justification lies not in theory but in practice, in the remarkable poetic effects which it can create. But it is above all meant to be *heard*. As Hopkins put it, sprung rhythm, 'once you hear it, is so eminently natural a thing and so effective a thing that if they [other poets] had known of it they would have used it'.

In a letter to his friend Robert Bridges Hopkins wrote that sprung rhythm 'lends itself to expressing passion'. On another occasion he wrote 'Feeling, love in particular, is the great moving power and spring of verse'. No doubt he felt that the coiled *spring* of feeling, the moving power of verse, could contain most stored energy when the rhythm too is *sprung*.

Hopkins's restless innovations were attempts to find new and more powerful means of expression. Poetic form, beautiful and satisfying though it can be, is not simply an end in itself, still less is it a set of arbitrary rules or merely decorative devices. It is a way of generating meaning. A known poetic form sets up expectations in the reader, expectations which are then either fulfilled or broken in practice. In this way poetry can contain far more precise indications about such things as tone of voice, emotion, or mood than are possible in prose. Thus poetry is a language with special resources of meaning not available elsewhere. It is language at its most highly organised and therefore most charged with meaning. Knowing that, Hopkins was constantly seeking ways of extending that power even further. In doing so he trod a fine line between innovation and convention, for if innovation goes too far, form itself is obscured and can no longer make its special contribution to meaning. The greatest impact is to be achieved by stretching poetic form to its limits while stopping just short of destroying it altogether. That is what Hopkins's poetry aims at.

2.4 INSCAPE

Hopkins coined the term inscape because there was no word in English which adequately suggested one of his most important ways of seeing the created world. His word perhaps bears some relation to words like 'landscape' or 'seascape'. Those are words which may suggest not just a visible scene but the way in which a visible scene can fall into a satisfying artistic composition, with a proper relation between the parts and the whole. 'Inscape' adapts this to refer to the inner order or form of any object.

Hopkins put it at its simplest when he wrote in a letter that inscape meant 'design' or 'pattern', and added that it was what he aimed at above all in poetry. When Hopkins uses the word in this sense he is showing a painter's or sketcher's interest in grasping the artistic law of an object's form. Some instances of how he used the word will make this clearer. Studying the shape of a horse, he wrote 'I looked at the groin or the flank and saw how the set of the hair symmetrically flowed outwards from it to all parts of the body, so that, following that one may inscape the whole beast very simply'. Here he uses inscape as a verb, meaning to recognise the single unifying principle of the horse's pattern. In many other examples he examines the most complex and changing sights in the natural world – rivers, mountains, trees, flowers, clouds – and seeks for analogies or metaphors which can pick out an order or design in apparently baffling or irregular shapes. Thus he notes that 'rushing streams may be described as inscaped ordinarily in pillows – and upturned troughs'. Or again, 'Even in withering the flower ran through beautiful inscapes by the screwing up of the petals into straight little barrels or tubes'. On holiday in Switzerland, he described the inscapes of the Little Matterhorn as 'a sharpened bolt rising from a flattened shoulder'. The comparisons he employs in these examples – pillows, troughs, barrels, tubes, a bolt, a shoulder – show how inscape is often a matter of analogy, to be grasped through metaphor or simile, and is therefore something which can be conveyed in poetry even to those who have not seen the particular object that Hopkins was looking at. He often uses the word inscape in his private writings, but never in his poetry, for in the poetry the important task is to put inscape into practice, to make the reader grasp the inscapes of particular things. The poem 'As kingfishers catch fire', however, comes close to expressing directly some of the ideas associated with inscape, and is a good introduction to the topic.

The care and particularity which Hopkins lavished on observing and describing the sights of the world is almost unparalleled in English poetry. He is always acutely aware that *this* cloud (or ash-tree, or bluebell) is unique and different from *that* one. Yet as we have seen, his concern with inscape is also an attempt to discover *general* properties and common features amid the infinite play of differences. Inscape may begin in close attention to what is individual or unique in an object, but it often ends in a grasping of its resemblances to other things, and hence its order or form or even its 'laws'.

Inscape, however, was not merely a visual matter concerned only with the surface appearance of things. For Hopkins it came to mean the inner essence of something, the foundation and support of its being and its individuality. In this way inscape became for Hopkins a religious idea as well as an artistic one. The more Hopkins remarks the infinite variety of all created objects, each one unique, the more he seeks for the half-hidden common feature. This corresponds exactly to his view of the relation between God and his creation, as we shall see in poems such as 'Pied Beauty'. The very variousness of created things, for Hopkins, only shows forth the singleness of their creator; the constant changeability of clouds or seas only reveals the changelessness of God. This, of course, would be regarded by many people as a paradox. Hopkins would rather have called it a mystery. As a devout Catholic Hopkins was quite at home with the idea that some of the most profound truths, which are matters of faith, cannot be demonstrated by logic or reason. His friend the poet Robert Bridges was a sceptic who lacked sympathy with his religion, and Hopkins once defined the difference between them as follows. To

Bridges, he said, a mystery was 'an interesting uncertainty', whereas to Hopkins himself it was 'an incomprehensible certainty'. In that remark one glimpses something of the strength of Hopkins's religious faith.

In the end, then, inscape is a concept which is upheld by faith: the faith that all created things, if seen properly, reveal their creator. With the simplicity of complete conviction Hopkins once expressed this as follows: 'I do not think I have ever seen anything more beautiful than the bluebell I have been looking at. I know the beauty of our Lord by it.' And immediately he went on to describe its inscape, in this case a mixture of 'strength and grace'.

I have argued that Hopkins often uses inscape to refer to the quality of similarity-within-difference, or order-within-randomness. But at other times he seems to use it to mean simply the essence of each created thing or being which makes it uniquely itself. So on one occasion he calls inscape 'species or individually-distinctive beauty of style'. Literally, of course, a species is a type: it exhibits difference when compared to all other species, but it exhibits similarity too in that all members of a given species have something in common. Yet at times Hopkins seemed to feel that each individual *member* of a species was, as it were, a species all of its own. He once said that originality in poetry is 'a condition of poetic genius; so that each poet is like a species in nature . . . and can never recur'.

It was natural for Hopkins to apply his idea of inscape not just to the natural world but to poetry too. 'Poetry is in fact speech only employed to carry the inscape of speech for the inscape's sake – and therefore the inscape must be dwelt on . . . repetition, *oftening, over-and-overing, aftering* of the inscape must take place in order to detach it to the mind and in this light poetry is speech which afters and oftens its inscape.' (What he meant by words such as 'aftering' and 'oftening' can best be understood by looking at the use of repetition in a poem such as 'Binsey Poplars'.) Verse, he concluded, is 'speech employed to carry the inscape of spoken sound'.

The term 'instress', closely related to inscape, is another of his coinages. By it he meant the internal force which holds inscapes together, as when he wrote 'all things are upheld by instress and are meaningless without it'. He also used it to mean the impression, or striking force, with which inscapes are conveyed to the beholder: thus, on seeing a comet, he wrote 'I felt a certain awe and instress, a feeling of strangeness'. He uses the word 'instress' (as a verb) once in his poetry, in stanza five of 'The Wreck of the Deutschland'.

2.5 IGNATIUS

St Ignatius Loyola, the sixteenth-century founder of the Jesuit order, wrote his *Spiritual Exercises* as a handbook of spiritual training. In constant use among all members of the Society of Jesus, they had a deep influence on Hopkins's life and art as he meditated upon them and practised the exercises they prescribe. They begin with the principle that 'Man was created to praise, reverence, and serve God our Lord, and by this means to save his soul'. Hence the motto of the Jesuits, 'Ad maiorem Dei gloriam' (to the greater glory of God). Hopkins submitted all his actions and writings to this test: anything which would not lead to the greater glory of God he did not do.

The Exercises prescribe a course of action covering four weeks, designed to be put into practice under the guidance of a spiritual director. The first stage is aimed at a rooting out of faults and sin. The second offers the example of Christ's perfection as a model to imitate, and culminates in a resolve to do so. The third stage confirms that resolution by a meditation on the Passion of Christ, and the fourth aims at union with God through love. At many points the Jesuit must use the power of imagination to enter fully into the situation which he is required to meditate upon, and must conduct a dialogue with God about it. Given this emphasis on the use of the imagination, it is clear that the techniques as well as the subjects of the *Spiritual Exercises* are reflected in many of Hopkins's poems.

As for nature and the other things of this world, Ignatius said that they were created to help man in his task of praising God and saving his soul. He ought to make use of them in so far as they will serve that end, but shun them in so far as they hinder it. Here lay a potential problem for Hopkins: his love of nature and beauty must not be allowed to become an end in itself, and was to be indulged only when it would lead him towards, not distract him from, God. How could he be certain that his endless fascination with nature in its minutest details was not a self-indulgence? And how could he reconcile the religious ideal of self-denial in the service of God with his view that all things strive for selfhood and individual perfection? The answers to such questions will become apparent below.

2.6 DUNS SCOTUS

Ideas attributable to the mediaeval philosopher and theologian Duns Scotus (1265–1308) occur in several of Hopkins's poems, and he figures large in the poem 'Duns Scotus's Oxford'. Hopkins discovered Scotus's writings in 1872, and reported himself 'flush with a new stroke of enthusiasm' as a result.

Three of Scotus's doctrines were important to Hopkins:
(1) The 'thisness', individuation, or uniqueness of all things and beings. Scotus's term for 'thisness' was the Latin word *haecceitas*. This emphasis on the distinguishing features of each particular thing may seem similar to Hopkins's idea of inscape. There is one important difference, however: *haecceitas* refers to the unique features which differentiate a thing from all other things, whereas

inscape, as we have seen, often refers to a distinctive pattern or 'law' of an object's being, and a pattern or law, by definition, is common to a number of things. Hopkins had formed his idea of inscape for himself before he ever read Scotus. The idea of 'thisness' is one part of Scotus's theory of knowledge. For most mediaeval philosophers, knowledge is of the intellect, not the senses, for it is easy to show that sense-perceptions can be unreliable. Now the senses deal in particulars, whereas the intellect deals in abstractions, categories, and universals. Because knowledge is of the intellect, only these latter things constitute knowledge: the registration of particular phenomena which the senses provide is not knowledge. Scotus challenged this view by insisting on the ability of the senses to provide direct knowledge of real things. What they enable us to know is the *haecceitas* of a thing, its particular combination of qualities which make it unique. For Hopkins, passionately devoted all his life to the delights of the eye and the ear, this vindication of the senses was cause for enthusiasm indeed.

(2) The Immaculate Conception of the Virgin Mary, that is, the belief that the mother of Christ, alone of all mortals, was free from the taint of Original Sin, that hereditary burden shared by all humankind and stemming from Adam's disobedience in the Garden of Eden and the Fall of Man.

(3) Scotus's unusual beliefs about the Incarnation of Christ. In his view, the Incarnation was not conceived of in the mind of God as a response to the Fall after it had happened. Rather, both the Fall and its redemption through the Incarnation were ordained long beforehand, at the Creation itself. It follows that the narrative of the Original Sin which produced the Fall, and the atonement for that sin by way of Christ's death on the cross, has meaning and value as a symbolic pattern. It is a sign of the symmetry of God's creative planning, and brings one close to admiring sin, and the suffering that it causes, for their own sakes, rather than seeing the sin as evidence of man's freedom to choose to turn away from God, and the sacrifice as evidence of God's freely given love for his erring creation. These are murky waters to all of us who are not theologians. But they may help to explain why 'The Wreck of the Deutschland', in the view of some readers, comes close to admiring suffering for the sake of suffering.

Hopkins may himself have suffered for his admiration of Scotus. We know that he fully expected to spend four years at St Beuno's in Wales studying theology, but that he left after three, much against his will. It is possible, though it remains a matter for speculation, that his superiors denied him the opportunity he wished for because they felt he was becoming too enamoured of Scotist doctrine. Though certainly not considered heretical, Scotus was clearly regarded with some reservations by nineteenth-century Jesuits. In Hopkins's view, 'he saw too far, he knew too much'.

Concerning mortal beauty, selfhood, and the things of the created world, Hopkins learned little that was new to him from Scotus. Rather, Scotus confirmed views which Hopkins had already arrived at for himself, and perhaps lent them some measure of respectability. With Scotus to support him, he became more than ever convinced that the infinite variety of the world only shows forth the singleness of its creator, and that the ideal of self-denial and self-abnegation which his religion placed before him need not be at odds with his passionate belief that selfhood and self-realisation is the aim of all things. The closer he studied the inscapes and the 'thisness' of things, the more he was seeing God's presence in the world and giving God that praise for which man was created.

3 'THE WRECK OF THE DEUTSCHLAND'

3.1 ORIGINS OF THE POEM

On Saturday 4 December 1875 a transatlantic steamship left her home port of Bremen in Germany carrying emigrants bound for New York. The *Deutschland* was a substantial ship, built at Greenock in Scotland, 328 feet long, drawing nearly 3000 tons, and was carrying about 120 passengers and 90 crew. At once she ran into heavy weather and spent the Saturday night sheltering in the mouth of the River Weser. On Sunday she headed for the English Channel. Darkness came early that day, and with it came driving snow and seas whipped up by the continuing gale. For twelve hours she drove on into the storm in very bad visibility. Captain Brickenstein had two experienced pilots beside him, six lookouts posted, and a seaman taking depth soundings with a lead line. At 4 a.m. he reduced speed and called for more frequent depth soundings. What none of them knew was that they were already many miles off course, driven by a following wind, and heading not into the Straits of Dover but towards the treacherous shoals of the outermost reaches of the Thames estuary.

Just after 5 a.m., peering through the whirling snow, they suddenly saw breakers ahead. The gale was carrying them rapidly towards a sandbank. The captain ordered full speed astern. The *Deutschland* shuddered under the strain, and a few moments later the propeller broke off. The ship drifted on to the sands of the Kentish Knock, bumping lightly twice and then becoming stuck fast. The lives of those on board the helpless ship now depended on rescue. Yet there was little immediate danger. Monday's dawn was not far away, and when it came the day was clear. Ships were passing, the shore was not far off, several lightships were in the vicinity, and the *Deutschland* signalled for help with rockets and pistols. As Monday drew on the passengers kept up their spirits. They had plenty to eat and drink, and the men busied themselves working the pumps while the crew laboured all day throwing cargo overboard to lighten the vessel. Yet the entire day went by without any attempt at rescue, even though their distress signals had been seen and answered from the shore. The seamen of Harwich later argued that they were unable to help because they did not have a lifeboat, yet they did not think to telegraph to any of the nearby towns which did.

Monday night drew on, the high winds continued, and the tide began to rise over the trapped ship. Gradually the cabins and saloons filled with water, and the passengers and crew were forced to clamber on top of the wheelhouse or into the rigging. The intense cold took its toll. One by one they lost their strength and were washed away.

An account of what happened during that night was to be read by Gerard Manley Hopkins and the rest of the nation a few days later in *The Times*. Their reporter wrote from Harwich:

After 3 a.m. on Tuesday morning a scene of horror was witnessed . . . Five German nuns, whose bodies are now in the dead-house here, clasped hands and were drowned together, the chief sister, a gaunt woman 6 ft. high, calling out loudly and often 'O Christ, come quickly!' till the end came . . . One brave sailor, who was safe in the rigging, went down to try and save a child or woman who was drowning on deck. He was secured by a rope to the rigging, but a wave dashed him against the bulwarks, and when daylight dawned his headless body, detained by the rope, was swaying to and fro with the waves. In the dreadful excitement of these hours one man hung himself behind the wheelhouse, another hacked at his wrist with a knife, hoping to die a comparatively painless death by bleeding.

It was eight in the morning before the tide retreated and the survivors could return to the decks. They waited several more hours before a tug from Harwich came alongside and took them to safety. By that time the *Deutschland* had been on the bank for thirty hours, and for at least half that time people on shore had known that a vessel was in distress and done nothing to help. Yet within minutes of the rescue a swarm of small boats pounced on the wreck and began looting anything movable, including money and rings from the corpses. It was these circumstances which turned a disaster into a national disgrace.

This, then, is the subject of Hopkins's longest and greatest single poem. As he says in stanza 24, he was in Wales when the news of the *Deutschland's* loss reached the nation. He was now in the second year of his theological studies at St Beuno's, and for seven years he had kept his self-imposed resolution not to spend energy on poetic composition. But this incident moved him greatly for several reasons. Always an ardent patriot, he shared in the national sense of shame.

And the subject had an imaginative and personal appeal: a lifelong interest in shipwrecks was something he had in common with the family whom he now saw so little of. Marine insurance was the daily business of his father, who had even written a little book giving advice to sea-captains about shipwrecks. His brothers Arthur and Everard were to spend their lives as professional artists, and shipwrecks were among their subjects. A few years later another of Hopkins's own poems, 'The Loss of the Eurydice', was also to concern a shipwreck.

Beyond this there was a powerful religious appeal. Five Catholic nuns, exiled from the land of their birth by oppressive legislation (the Falck laws, which Hopkins mentions in the poem's subtitle, sought to subordinate church to state), had been left to die by the people of Hopkins's own country. 'Rhine refused them, Thames would ruin them' as he puts it in stanza 21. And they had gone to their deaths in the most dramatic way, clasped together while one of them, herself a striking figure, called on Christ to come to them. Hopkins talked of it with one of his superiors at St Beuno's. That man, perhaps by chance or perhaps showing tactful understanding of Hopkins, said that he wished someone would write a poem about it. Hopkins needed no further prompting: his superior's remark released him from his scruples as to whether poetry was a fitting way for him to serve the greater glory of God. He began writing almost at once, and was working on the poem through the early months of 1876.

And yet it is not quite true to say that the shipwreck is *the* subject of the poem. As Hopkins wrote in a letter, 'The Deutschland would be more generally interesting if there were more wreck and less discourse, I know, but still it is an ode and not primarily a narrative.' Since the beginnings of the Western literary tradition, the ode has provided an opportunity for meditation, reflection, or philosophical discourse upon a great subject. This, not the mere relation of a series of events, is its purpose. The principle business of an ode is lyrical, not narrative. The wreck itself, then, was intended to be the occasion of the poem rather than its whole subject. And a glance at the poem shows that this is so: in Part the First, the opening ten stanzas, nothing is said about the shipwreck at all. Only at stanza 12 does narration of events begin, and from then on narration is interrupted several times until it finally gives way altogether to the other business of the poem. Just what that other business is will become clearer as we read on.

3.2 PART THE FIRST

Hopkins seized the chance to write his first major poem in sprung rhythm, which he said had long been 'haunting' his ear. Some of the poetic effects which this makes possible have already been explored in that section of this book which deals with sprung rhythm. But the precise scheme which Hopkins uses in 'The Wreck' needs noting here. As explained earlier, in sprung rhythm one line is like another, metrically speaking, if they contain the same number of stresses. But for the sake of variety Hopkins had no wish to make every line in the poem metrically identical to every other. So he devised a stanza form in which the lengths of the lines vary within the stanza, but each stanza is constructed on the same form as every other. Thus there is variety within each stanza but unity across all the stanzas, which conforms to Hopkins's ideas about the twin principles of artistic beauty. The scheme is this: in each stanza in Part the First, the different lines have the following number of stresses:

line number	number of stresses
1	2
2	3
3	4
4	3
5	5
6	5
7	4
8	6

The reader is reminded of this by the layout of the poem on the page, in which lines begin further to the left the more stresses they have. The only difference in Part the Second is that the first line of each stanza has three stresses instead of two, as can again be seen by a glance at the typography. It will help in grasping the rhythm of the poem if we remember that it is meant to be read aloud with firm emphasis on the stresses. This is where Hopkins probably intended them to fall in stanza 1:

> Thóu mastering mé
> , God! giver of breáth and breád;
> World's stránd, swáy of the séa;
> Lórd of living and deád;
> Thou hast bound bónes and veins in me, fástened me flésh,
> And áfter it álmost únmade, whát with dreád,
> Thy dóing: and dóst thou touch me afrésh?
> Óver agáin I féel thy finger and find thée.

The opening stanza stresses God's power as creator of the world and as giver and taker-away of life. God *is* the sway of the sea, as well as having sway over it. A swaying sea is uneasy or threatening to human beings, even though it is an instance of God's power. And God is also the world's strand, which might suggest a safe arrival on shore, but also reminds us of the stranded and wrecked ship. This emphasis on God's power and its dual nature foreshadows much that is to come later in the poem. Yet for the moment that power is a matter between God and the poet himself. In the first line, 'Thou mastering me', the stresses are on 'thou' and 'me': already Hopkins is using the resources of sprung rhythm to create meaning. The intensely personal relationship between the creator and his creature is emphasised again in the last line of stanza 1, with its stress on 'thee'.

In fact much of Part the First is to be a personal account of the poet's own actual past experiences in his dealings with God. Writing about the poem in a letter to his friend Bridges, Hopkins said 'what refers to myself in the poem is all strictly and literally true and did all occur; nothing is added for poetical padding'. This seems to apply in particular to the second and third stanzas with their account of a terrifying but ultimately comforting spiritual encounter. Perhaps Hopkins is writing here of some episode connected with his decision to become a priest or to join the Jesuits, perhaps of some other crisis in his religious life. The exact biographical details are unimportant, because they are not stated: it is enough that God knows where and when this occurred (stanza 2, line 5). What matters is the imagery here, of stress and terror, of a desperate search for release ('where, where was a, where was a place?') followed by the recognition at the end of stanza 3 that God, the source of his terror, is also his means of escape from that terror. His heart, he says, had the intuition needed to realise this: 'carrier-witted' means that it had the homing instincts of a carrier pigeon. The difficult last line of stanza 3 uses the same words, 'flame' and 'grace', to refer both to the terror he was trying to escape from and to the comfort he was trying to reach. Both were God. That apparent paradox – that God is both terrifying and loving, both destructive and merciful – is one which we already noticed in the first stanza. It will recur often, and will take us close to the heart of the poem's meaning. One of its clearest appearances is in stanza 9:

Thou art lightning and love, I found it, a winter and warm

In that line the apparently contradictory qualities of God are linked with 'and' rather than the more usual 'but'. This is a way of insisting that both kinds of quality are equally present and suggesting that the paradox of God's nature is not something that can be grasped by ordinary common sense or logic.

The beautiful fourth stanza uses three different images to define the poet's inner state. The first four lines compare that state to sand in an hourglass, crumbling and falling, 'mined' from underneath though apparently stable at the edge. In the next line, the image is of water smooth as a pane of glass, but the word 'poise' suggests that this equilibrium is only a momentary balance of forces. The third image is of a perilous descent: 'voel' (pronounced 'voyl') is a Welsh word for a mountain. All that supports him is the rope provided by faith and grace, God's revelation of himself through the gospels and his presence in man through Christ.

In line 5 of stanza 4 'steady', often an adjective, is used as a verb, and in the last line 'proffer', normally a verb, becomes a noun. This is typical of Hopkins's use of language. Here it is a way of suggesting that the active, dynamic qualities which we associate with verbs are also present in the apparently stable states which we usually name with nouns or adjectives, and vice versa. The device is particularly appropriate in this stanza, because all three main images show that his spiritual state is a fluid one, a perilous balance between collapse (like the sand or the mountaineer) and stability.

The fifth stanza turns to another way besides the gospel and the Incarnation in which God reveals himself, and it is Hopkins's favourite one in his poetry. In the stars, the thunder, and the sunset ('dappled-with-damson west') he recognises the beauty and the power of God. But God does more than just reveal himself: he is actually present in his creation. The poet *understands* that God *stands under* the 'splendour and wonder'. In this stanza Hopkins uses the word 'instressed' for the only time in his poetry: see the section of this book on inscape and instress. In the context it seems to mean to recognise the internal force which holds inscapes together (because of God's presence in them) and then to dwell on or proclaim ('stress') it. Perhaps, too, the phrase 'instressed, stressed' corresponds with the phrase 'a pressure, a principle' in the previous stanza. Otherwise this stanza is one of the easier parts of the poem. Hopkins takes care to provide these interludes. What follows is harder.

Stanzas six to eight form a single unit of thought. We may begin the sixth stanza in the middle. 'Stars and storms' restates the now-familiar point about the beauty and terror of God being inseparable. We might associate the 'stress' of line 2 with the instressing of the beauty of such things as stars in the previous stanza; and the 'stroke' of line 4 with punishment or terror (though a stroke can be a tender caress as well as a fierce blow). But now, in the line

Stroke and a stress that stars and storms deliver

the order of words suggests that 'stroke' goes with 'stars' and 'stress' with 'storms'. God's beauty belongs to the storms as much as the stars; his power to the stars as much as the storms. Hopkins says that the stress and the stroke do not come 'out of his bliss' nor 'first from heaven', and that this is known to few. Just what this means is a matter for argument. But we notice that 'it' in line 7 of stanza 6 must refer to stroke and stress: they are now being thought of as a single, interchangeable 'it'. And the same 'it' recurs right through stanzas 7 and 8 as the subject of the thought. Stanza 7 says that 'it', whatever it is, dates from Christ's life and death on earth. In two compact lines, 'Manger, maiden's knee' and 'The dense and the driven Passion, and frightful sweat', Hopkins sketches that momentous life from beginning to end. This was God's greatest manifestation of love for his world. And from that came 'the discharge of it', its 'swelling', metaphors which suggest an electrical shock and a steady growth. Hopkins, then, is talking about the effect upon the world of Christ's incarnation, and of God's love for his creation.

Stanza 8, as its last lines show, is about the union of man with God. The way in which that union comes about is not through something 'known' (see the last line of Stanza 7) but through the sudden, intuitive leap of the loving heart. Before it makes its leap the heart, separate from God, is suffering, 'hard at bay'. And the leap involves the risk of further suffering, for the sloe of stanza 8 is a fruit which may be either sweet or intensely bitter: only by running the risk of bursting it in the mouth can one have the chance of obtaining sweetness.

We must now review the meaning of stanzas 6 to 8. It is God's love, discharged upon the world in the life of Christ, which has the power to draw people suddenly and unawares to God. But this same love or power is also possessed by the 'stroke' and 'stress' delivered by the 'stars and storms', for they too, according to stanza 6, hush guilt and flush or melt hearts. It seems that God's love, his power, and his presence in the world are all being spoken of as one and the same thing. For Hopkins, God's presence in the world is perpetual and everywhere: we see this in stanza 5 and in many of his other poems. He seems to be saying that God's love and power are equally perpetual and omnipresent: in stanza 6 'it rides time like riding a river'. The stroke does not come 'first from heaven', not directly from God, but rather through Christ's incarnation. Nor does the stress come 'out of his bliss' but rather out of Christ's suffering. In other words, it is wrong to think of God as sitting in heaven making only the occasional intervention in the world, according to his mood, as it were. Rather, God is perpetually present *in man* as much as in the stars and the storms, and has been ever since Christ became man. As Hopkins once put it, 'that is Christ playing at me and me playing at Christ'. This emphasis on Christ as a living man comes in the seventh of the ten stanzas of Part the First. If we glance ahead to the corresponding point in Part the Second, seven-tenths of the way through it, we come to stanza 28. There Christ is asked – perhaps – to make another appearance on earth.

Stanzas 9 and 10 are easier. The hymn to God in stanza 9 emphasises the now-familiar point that he is 'most . . . merciful' even in the midst of 'dark', or 'wrecking and storm'. By these means our attitude to the shipwreck has been prepared well before the narrative itself begins. Stanza 10 is a wish that man in general may be converted to God's will. St Paul's conversion was a sudden one (conveyed powerfully by the sprung rhythms of 'at a crash Paul'); St Augustine's was gradual: never mind how, says Hopkins, but let it happen 'in all of us'. So ends Part the First, with a stress on God as 'King', just as Part the Second will end with a stress on 'Lord'.

The first part of the poem, like the rest, is full of startling poetic effects achieved by the careful organisation of language. We notice Hopkins's habit of taking conventional phrases staled by over-use and jerking them back into life: in stanza 2 'O Christ' sounds like a profane oath, just as in stanza 7 'frightful sweat' sounds casual, until we realise that Hopkins is taking these phrases literally and so showing that even our thoughtless remarks contain more truth, more evidence of Christ, than we are usually aware of. Notice, too, effects of immediacy such as 'Brim, in a flash, full!' (stanza 8) where a departure from normal word-order is used to inscape an instantaneous moment and suggest something which happens more quickly than we can usually say it.

Then there are the effects which come from the careful patterning of vowels and consonants, as for instance in stanza 8 in the sequence of words 'lash . . . lush . . . plush . . . flesh . . . Gush . . . flush . . . flash', sounds which suggest the tactile qualities of the fruit bursting upon the palate. And there is the form of the stanza, with its challenging rhyme-scheme *ababcbca*. The *a* rhymes at beginning and end bring each stanza full-circle, and Hopkins usually reinforces this effect by putting a major pause in the sense at the end of each stanza, so that they become complete units in themselves. But in poetry, once a regular expectation such as that has been set up, it stands ready to be broken, so creating surprise, and Hopkins does so by running stanza 7 straight on into stanza 8 and thereby suggesting the sudden, unexpected way in which the heart, with its intuitive wisdom and love, leaps to God.

3.3 PART THE SECOND

As Part the Second opens in stanza 11 we hear words spoken by Death itself. With the narrative of the shipwreck about to begin, it seems appropriate that Death should have the first word, for it is not to have the last. 'Some [people] find me [in the form of] a sword' is the meaning of the first line: Hopkins always omits unnecessary words in order to make his language as energetic as possible. If that means that the reader has to work harder, the price is usually worth paying.

All the images in this stanza are of violent deaths, just as the shipwreck was. 'The flange and the rail' refers not to individual suicides lying in the path of an oncoming train but to the multiple deaths caused by derailment. Perhaps Hopkins was thinking of the railway accident at Abbots Ripton on 21 January 1876, only six weeks after the loss of the *Deutschland*, which, by a remarkable series of coincidences, also involved a collision caused by a north-east gale, blinding snow, and men who ignored urgent messages which might have saved lives. The 'scythe' and the 'share' are the traditional images associated with Death the Reaper. Man, says the poem, forgets the fate that awaits him. There is a hint here that one good consequence of such disasters is to remind us of our end and of the life to come.

Hopkins said that the next few stanzas were among 'the best and most intelligible' in the poem, and they present few difficulties. At the end of stanza 12 he thinks of those on the ship who, as Protestants perhaps, were not themselves aware of being under God's wing ('feathers') and, in a rhetorical question, feels sure that his infinite mercy was available to 'reeve' (rope in) them too. In stanza 13 sprung rhythm at its most rapid combines with onomatopoeia in the line

Wiry and white-fiery and whirlwind-swivelled snow

Even the words 'unchilding unfathering', which point to the grim losses suffered by families, perhaps contain a hint of God's presence, for, to a Christian, God is a father and people are his children in a way that death cannot alter.

In stanza 14 Hopkins includes for the first time one of his oddest poetic techniques. Line 1 as usual rhymes with line 3, but the actual rhyming sounds are 'leeward' (pronounced 'looard') and 'drew her/ D . . . '. The rhyme is not complete till the first consonant of line 4. The same technique occurs several more times later in the poem. Hopkins no doubt felt that if rhythm could be 'rove-over' from one line to the next in order to bind them more tightly together, why not rhyme too? The risk here is that in English poetry the more contrived a rhyme appears, the more it verges upon the humorous, as when, for example, Byron writes in his great comic epic *Don Juan*

But – Oh! ye lords of ladies intellectual,
Inform us truly, have they not hen-pecked you all?

Some of the rhymes in 'The 'Wreck of the Deutschland' are perilously similar to such a comic effect: in stanza 31 'Providence' is rhymed to 'of it and/ S . . . ' But Hopkins was never afraid to take risks in his poetry.

The 'whorl' in stanza 14 is in the ship's broken propeller: she had sails too, hence 'canvas'. Most of the details in this part of the poem closely follow the newspaper reports quoted earlier, and with them in mind stanzas 14 to 17 should be self-explanatory at a first reading. But the language is characteristic of Hopkins, such as (in stanza 16) 'braids of thew' to describe the roped and plaited muscles of the sailor, or the word 'burl', suggesting the heaving and spinning violence of the wind.

At the end of stanza 17 the cries of the sufferers on the ship are interrupted by the voice of the tall nun, whose strength of purpose and clarity of understanding are suggested by the words 'lioness' and 'prophetess' respectively. Her words are of such significance that they interrupt the narrative too. In fact they put an end to it. For from this moment onwards the entire second half of the poem concerns itself with the meaning of her words (they are not quoted until stanza 24) and actions, or with the thoughts which they provoke in the poet. From him in turn 'words break' forth: words are mentioned often in the poem, and in a way which suggests their power and significance. The suggestion is that both nun and poet are faintly echoing in their own way the all-creating Word of God.

And so in stanza 18 Hopkins turns to address his own heart, just as he had done in stanza 3: there are many such links or parallels between the two parts of the poem. Stanza 18 is about the overwhelming feelings which caught him unawares at the thought of the nun's words, and it is worth analysing in detail how Hopkins achieves his emotional effects here. It is done in part by his invariably choosing surprising and effective words such as 'madrigal', and in part by the way those words are then linked to each other more closely than one would have thought possible. For instance in the phrase 'never-eldering revel' the noun consists entirely of sounds borrowed from the preceding compound adjective and rearranged. At times it seems as if each word in a Hopkins poem is attempting to generate the word which follows it. That is why despite the frequent strangeness of his language there is also a sense of inevitability and rightness about it. But emotional effects are also created by rhythm and syntax. Consider the first four lines of the stanza:

> Ah, tóuched in your bówer of bóne ,
> Are you! turned for an éxquisite smárt,
> Have you! máke words bréak from me hére all alóne,
> Do you! – móther of béing in me, héart.

Here, 'Are you!', 'Have you!', and 'Do you!' are all unstressed, and enjambed (that is, with the sense run on without a pause) from the previous line. The effect is to make the reader literally run short of breath as he tries to articulate phrases which trail away and unexpectedly prolong the utterance. But those same phrases, because word-order has been inverted, complete the sense of the previous line, so that meaning falls surprisingly into place at the last moment. It amounts to a remarkably effective way of making the reader enact a repeated sigh, or a catch in the voice, as if almost choked by a sudden access of emotion. That emotion is an 'exquisite smart', a pain which is also a joy and a 'glee', and which comes from contemplating the nun's suffering but also her strength and faith. This mixture reminds us again of the paradox of God's nature which has been emphasised throughout.

In stanza 19 we find Hopkins coining words (neologisms) to inscape the power of violent seas. 'Hawling' and 'sloggering' each come packed with several meanings: the first suggests words such as howling, hauling, hurling; the second seems to be 'slogging' and 'slobbering' rolled into one. More difficult is the 'one fetch' which 'she [in] that weather' has in her. It may simply mean 'effort'; it also has an appropriate nautical sense, meaning to tack; but Hopkins was aware that 'fetch' can also mean 'wraith', 'apparition', 'spectre'. Perhaps her single-mindedness is really a manifestation of the Holy Spirit working within her. Certainly she is already close to God, for she raises her cry to 'divine ears'. Having planted these hints, Hopkins now lays aside the question of the nun's meaning until stanza 24, and stanzas 20 to 23 are meditative. Though an interlude, this is no digression. Such 'discourse', as Hopkins called it, is a way of expanding the theme and is of the essence of an ode. He begins in stanza 20 by contemplating the fate of all five nuns. His own knowledge of the wreck was at second hand: all he had were words and names: yet, given the God-like power of words, that was more than enough, and here it is the words themselves which lead him on. Stanza 20 revolves around names, just as stanza 22 will elaborate upon the significances of the word 'five'. 'Deutschland' is a doubly desperate name because it belongs both to the fatal ship and to the country from which they had to flee. This reminds the poet that Germany's threats to Catholicism are not new: Luther, 'beast of the waste wood', was an instigator of the Protestant Reformation. But at once he finds further evidence of the strangely close kinship of good and evil in the world, for St Gertrude, he remembers, was born in the same small town as Luther.

As in stanza 20 the good and evil *of the world* are twins, so in stanza 21 the evils of the world are intricately connected with the goodness of God in heaven. Many writers have been struck by the meaninglessness of evil, but Hopkins is not among them: he sees the suffering of the nuns as a test or trial, an opportunity for them to demonstrate the strength of their faith, akin to that of martyrdom. God here is Orion the hunter, seeking out good and evil. He is also a judge, whose 'poising palms' are 'weighing the worth' of his people. Seen in this way the storm has its own beauty, described in the last two lines of the stanza which depend upon Hopkins's central conviction that God is actually present in his world, whether in storms or in flowers. The word 'unchancelling', another of Hopkins's coinages, is itself poised between these two different meanings, for it may suggest, on the one hand, that the nuns have been removed from the oppressive power of the German Chancellor Bismarck; but, on the other, that they have been driven out of the safety of the church's chancel in order to face a sterner test. The same word, then, may stand equally for a welcome liberation or a terrifying struggle: in this poem those two things are indistinguishable.

Stanza 22 takes up some of the traditional and symbolic meanings of the number five. From the five nuns he turns to the five wounds (the stigmata) of Christ on the cross, but the connection between nuns and Christ does not depend arbitrarily on the number alone, for their suffering, faith, and death echos his. Here is another link with Part the First, where the Passion was mentioned in stanza 7. Just as the tall nun will later be praised for her power to 'read' correctly the meaning concealed in the 'unshapeable shock night' (stanza 29) so here Hopkins is busy reading or interpreting: stanza 22 is crowded with words which denote *signs*, such as 'cipher', 'mark', 'stigma', 'signal', 'token', 'lettering'. Even 'sake', another of Hopkins's favourite words, suggests outward and visible signs, for he once explained it as meaning 'the being a thing has outside itself', something distinctive by which it is recognisable. To a Christian these are the outward and visible signs of an inward and spiritual grace. But to a poet, this emphasis on reading and interpreting signs demonstrates how this poem is concerned with the construction of meaning. Its subject is not so much the wreck as the meaning of the wreck. That meaning is not waiting, fixed and unproblematic, within the story of the wreck. It has to be produced by interpretation. Being a human production, meaning may be misproduced, as in stanza 6 by those who 'fable and miss'. 'The Wreck of the Deutschland' forces its readers to work hard to construct its meanings. But that is entirely appropriate for a poem where the subject, in part, is just this business of the way meanings have to be *sought*.

Stanza 23 continues with the association of ideas. St Francis too carried the five stigmata as a sign of his intense devotion to Christ, and the five drowned nuns were Franciscans. The word 'lovescape', like inscape, suggests the internal nature of something (in this case God) made visible. By now the number five has taken on overtones of mystical significance, binding together nuns, Christ, and St Francis into a closer union, and so suggesting that the nuns' deaths had meaning, in being a recapitulation of those earlier lives and deaths. Even if Hopkins's theology should fail to convince us that the nuns' deaths were a welcome and blessed joining with God, the *poetic* logic of the more-than-coincidental fives has prepared the way for the end of stanza 23 where the nuns are immersed, so to speak, in God. In that remarkable last line the issue is confronted boldly, for the metaphors 'bathe' and 'breathe' risk being interpreted very literally when we think of a drowning. Without trying to minimise the physical horror of their fate, Hopkins is insisting that their metaphorical 'immersion' in God is more important than their literal drowning.

In stanza 24 Hopkins contrasts his own security at St Beuno's, in its idyllic pastoral setting, with the peril of those on the ship. This personal note is another link with Part the First, and indeed the nun's response to crisis – to reach out for grace and mercy – is the same as his was in stanzas 2 and 3. His 'flash from the flame to the flame', recognising that God was both the cause and the means of escape from his terror, is now paralleled by her calling her 'cross' (burden) by the name of Christ and understanding that 'her wild-worst' is really 'Best'. Hopkins, of course, says not only that she 'calls' but that she 'christens': the very act of naming is an acknowledgment of Christ. And, returning to the matter first raised in stanza 17, he quotes the words of the tall nun – though he does not go to the lengths of quoting them in the original German. It is her *meaning* which interests him, and the next four stanzas are to be devoted to considering just what she did mean.

Stanza 25 begins that consideration by calling upon the holy spirit ('arch and original Breath') for help. What *did* she mean when she called upon Christ to come quickly? Was it that she wanted to be 'as her lover had been', in other words to emulate Christ's death? Implicitly the answer given is no. Not even the disciples, 'the men [who] / Woke thee', thought that way; for in an identical situation, facing the prospect of death by drowning on the Sea of Galilee, they called on Christ to save, not martyr, them. Or was it that she simply wanted release from her suffering and would welcome death as a 'comfort' after the 'combating'? This second conjecture about her possible meaning closes stanza 25, but it is not answered till the start of stanza 27.

Stanza 26 is an interlude in the middle of these urgent questions which are driving the poem towards a climax of excitement. When mist or cloud ('the down-dugged ground-hugged grey') clears away, it reveals the beauty of the heavens, either by day or by night. The *visual* beauty of heaven (inscaped in the language here) is quite enough to cheer the heart. The real *substance* of heaven, then, which 'never eyesight got', must be more desirable still, to a degree immeasurable by human beings who cannot yet know it. Given that it is so natural to long for such a heaven, Hopkins implies, perhaps that was indeed what the tall nun meant: that she would have welcomed death. Again the answer is no, at the start of stanza 27. It is 'time's tasking' which gives rise to ('fathers') the heart's 'asking for ease': in other words, we tend to cry for release not at moments of high danger and crisis but after being worn down by prolonged trials. This is the reason for now answering no to the question which was posed at the end of stanza 25. What is more, the 'appealing of the Passion' is likewise greatest not during danger but in times of quiet meditation and prayer such as those prescribed in the *Spiritual Exercises*. So the answer to the *first* question of stanza 25, whether the tall nun was seeking to emulate Christ's death, must be no too, as we had already suspected from the point about the disciples.

This long exploration of the meaning of the nun's cry now reaches its own crisis. Having rejected two interpretations of her words, stanza 27 ends on an apparently enigmatic note, saying simply that she meant something else: 'her mind's / Burden' was 'other' than those just discussed. We therefore expect that the next stanza, 28, will at last declare exactly what she did mean by 'O Christ, Christ, come quickly'. But stanza 28 says nothing more, at least overtly, about her words. So stanza 28 must contain the answer implicitly, otherwise Hopkins would be teasing the reader with an anti-climax, frustrating the carefully-prepared expectation that we will finally find out what she meant. Everything about stanza 28 suggests that it is a moment of unusually high tension. Up till now the poem has shown extraordinary control over its language and syntax (indeed its apparent oddities of expression are mostly the result of the language being *more highly* controlled and patterned than is usual in everyday speech and writing). But now, at the start of stanza 28, syntax collapses, the poet's powers of articulacy seem to fail, and all we hear are broken phrases. Some of those phrases suggest the poet searching for adequate means of expression ('But how shall I . . . ') and calling for inspiration ('Fancy, come faster'). Others seem to be snatches of speech from the shipwreck. This is a way of suggesting that the poet's confusion and crisis matches that of those on board the ship. And the words 'Fancy, come faster' contain a significant echo of 'Christ, come quickly': the poet's cry and the nun's are essentially the same.

At last, it seems, the nun's cry is answered. The 'sight' which looms turns out to be Christ, and he is named over and over again for emphasis: 'the Master,/ *Ipse*, the only one, Christ, King, Head'. Hopkins believed in using foreign words as sparingly as possible in his poetry: here he uses the Latin *ipse* presumably because there is no single word in English exactly equivalent to its meaning, which is 'he himself'. At the same time the poet's cry is answered too. 'What did she mean?', he had asked. It now seems that in calling on Christ to come quickly the nun meant something startlingly simple and literal: she wanted Christ to *be with her* there and then, no more and no less. Often in his poetry Hopkins likes taking things literally, at face value. For all his ingenuity, he also delights in the simple and straightforward, even the naive, meanings of words.

In the sixth line of stanza 28 we are reminded once again that God, or Christ, is both the cause of 'extremity' and the one to 'cure' it. In the next line, the verbs 'do, deal, lord it' *might* be governed, like 'cure', by 'He was to . . . '. Or they might go with the following line's 'Let him . . . '. In any case, the poem does not say 'he did': it says, first, 'He was to . . . do', and then 'Let him . . . do'. The crucial importance of this will become clear in a moment.

Though stanza 28 is by no means the most difficult in the poem, it is the one which has aroused most controversy in recent years. In her book *The Dragon in the Gate* the critic Elisabeth Schneider argued that Hopkins was claiming a miracle here by suggesting that what the nun saw was no mere vision of Christ but the real presence of Christ himself. Some readers have found this interpretation hard to accept. In my view Hopkins is certainly suggesting something more real than a mere vision or illusion on the part of the nun. The emphasis in stanza 28 is on Christ himself, in person as it were, and in that way it is quite in keeping with the stress which we have found throughout the poem on God's presence in his world. But this does not mean that he was necessarily claiming a miracle in the sense of something out of the natural order of things. Quite the reverse, in fact: for Hopkins God's presence in the world is a commonplace, everyday miracle. What some critics tend to forget, at this crucial moment, is that Hopkins's poem is not primarily a narrative. Nowhere in stanza 28 or later does the poem say 'this happened'. Rather it says 'let it happen', or 'let it have happened'. (Hopkins expresses the same wish about the past at the beginning of 'Henry Purcell', where he hopes that God may have allowed Purcell to be saved: as a mere mortal, Hopkins cannot know whether this had in fact happened or not.) At the end of stanza 28 of 'The Wreck' and again in stanzas 34 and 35, the verbs are in the imperative, not the indicative mood (stanza 28: 'Let him ride . . . in his triumph'; stanza 34: 'Now burn'; stanza 35: 'Let him easter in us'). The poem is dealing with fervent hopes and wishes, not with facts nor with claims about particular actions of Christ's.

Stanza 29, like stanza 22, is full of images about signs, words, interpretation, and meaning. The tall nun is praised for her skill in being able to 'read' the apparently 'unshapeable' events of that night and for 'wording' them correctly, in other words recognising Christ in them and naming him accordingly. She has a 'single eye', desiring Christ for himself alone and not for any benefit he may confer. How else should she name the storm but by the name of God, who himself 'worded' (created by his word) present and past, heaven and earth? In this way the nun is rock-fast ('Simon Peter' and 'Tarpeian' both suggest rocks) in her faith and her power to understand, just as the poet understood in stanza 5 that God is 'under the world's splendour and wonder'.

Stanza 30 reflects upon another apparent coincidence just as striking as the numerous fives of stanzas 22 and 23. The 'feast' which 'followed the night' of the wreck was that of the 'one woman without stain', free from the taint of original sin: December the 8th is the

Feast of the Immaculate Conception of the Virgin Mary. This doctrine of the Immaculate Conception was important to Hopkins: see the sections of this book on Duns Scotus and on the poem 'Duns Scotus's Oxford'. Just as Mary was conceived without sin, and in turn conceived Christ, so the nun's brain now conceives and gives birth to the 'Word' which is God.

Stanza 31 turns from considering the happy fate of the nun, who has her reward in Christ, to pity the others on board, 'comfortless' because 'unconfessed', still with their sins unforgiven, and therefore lacking God's grace. It is not their deaths but the fate of their souls after death which is bitter. But Hopkins can imagine a means for their salvation and hence their comfort. The nun's heart ('breast of the/Maiden'), by its obedience, could become an example to the others, like a bell to startle them back to God. In contrast to the violence of the storm, this touch of Providence is a thing of tender and feathery delicacy. (The effects of sprung rhythm in this line have been discussed above.) So the shipwreck could have become a 'harvest' of saved souls. Again Hopkins leaves this as a suggestion, for the stanza ends not with an assertion but with a question.

After these stanzas of reflection the poem now begins to move to its conclusion with two stanzas in praise of God, beginning with no. 32. He is in the tides and the 'gulf's sides' as he is in the 'wall' which restrains them. Unchanging himself, he is master of all which changes, such as the tides and the fall of the seasons. He is present now as he was long ago in the 'Yore-flood' (the Biblical deluge). Some of these images remind us of 'World's strand, sway of the sea' in stanza 1. And the fifth line of stanza 32 with its 'motionable mind' recalls stanza 4, the 'hourglass' stanza, where too the speaker was 'mined with a motion'. God is the 'granite' which can give a sure foundation to the spiritual uncertainty and instability of man. Likewise in the next stanza, 33, God's mercy and love is called a 'vein' which offers life to those who might seem in a hopeless case, past prayer or unrepentant till their last breath. This echoes the 'vein of the gospel proffer' from stanza 4. Hopkins is adding symmetry and shape to his poem by making the end recall the beginning. The syntax in lines 2 to 4 is 'an ark . . . for the lingerer with a love [which] glides/ Lower than death'. Christ is the giant who was plunged in passion (another reference to the crucifixion) and then rose from the dead: that promise of the life after death was shown forth in Christ and is likewise offered to the drowned.

Stanza 34 continues with the hopes, wishes, and pleas of stanza 28. Let Christ's name now burn again in the world, let it be reborn. That name is double-natured in that he was both God ('heaven-flung') and man ('heart-fleshed'). Again the poem stresses naming, for the nun's wisdom was in recognising and naming Christ. Numbering, like naming, is another way of recognising and identifying: Christ is 'mid-numberèd . . . in three', the second person of the Holy Trinity (Father, Son, Holy Spirit). Yet to name these things, though it may seem a clear and unequivocal act of recognition, is also to acknowledge a mystery, for the images in this stanza point to the aspects of God which defy human understanding: Christ is both man and God, God is one and three at the same time. Similarly, the line

Mid-numberèd He in three of the thunder-throne!

with its multiple alliterations verging on onomatopoeia, suggests Christ's power, like a roll of drums or peal of thunder; but the images which follow show that that power is combined with its apparent opposite: he is 'kind', a 'released shower' and not just 'a lightning of fire'.

The Bible tells of two appearances of Christ on earth, the first in his obscure birth and life as a man ('dark as he came'), the second at the end of time in the Last Judgment ('dooms-day dazzle'). The plea here and in the final stanza is for a third: that Christ may come to rule his kingdom on earth here and now, just as the nun had asked him to be with her in the here and now. Nothing could be more natural and proper, for a passionate lover of Christ such as Hopkins was, to wish for and even imagine the reign of Christ on earth. But there is a difference between wishing for it and claiming that it is under way. There are hints that the nun's magnificent example may tend to promote the kingdom of God in the hearts of human beings; but that, in my view, is as far as the poem goes in the direction of prophecy.

Stanza 35, with its triumphant tone and powerful orchestration, links the drowned nun and Christ for the last time. In both the first and the second lines, sprung rhythm demands a stress on 'our', recalling again the English disgrace of the failure to rescue the shipwrecked, and preparing for the words 'English' and 'Britain' later in the stanza. Because of the wreck, Christ is all the more needed amid the 'dimness' of Hopkins's loved country. But because of it too, he is, perhaps, all the more likely to come, to 'easter in us' (arise, or return to life, within people's hearts).

The poem began with an account of how Hopkins himself had come to dedicate himself to the service of God, and it ends with praise to God. That echos many a Jesuit piece of writing which begins with the motto 'Ad maiorem Dei gloriam' (to the greater glory of God) and ends with 'Laus Deo Semper' (praise to God always). The final symmetry which the poem contains is revealed when we look at its very first word – 'Thou' – and its very last – 'Lord'. In one sense, the entire meaning of 'The Wreck of the Deutschland' is contained inside that phrase: 'Thou [art] Lord'.

What we might call paradox, and what Hopkins called mystery, has been emphasised throughout the poem. The greatest paradox is that the horror and shame of the shipwreck is also a triumph: certainly a triumph for the tall nun, with her strength of faith and clarity of understanding; perhaps potentially a way to triumph for many others, through leading them to God. Disaster has been transformed into victory. Even for those readers who do not themselves believe in the Christian victory over death, the poetic logic of 'The Wreck of the Deutschland' is strong enough to make that transformation imaginatively convincing.

4 THE WELSH SONNETS

Between February and September 1877, the final months of his three years at St Beuno's College in North Wales, Hopkins wrote ten sonnets which are one of the high points of his poetic achievement. In calling them the Welsh Sonnets I mean to suggest that these poems can be considered as a group. They are bound together by the chronology of their composition and the fact that many of them draw upon Hopkins's experiences in Wales. They also show many similarities of poetic technique and theme.

'God's Grandeur'

The poem opens with a metaphor – 'charged' – of electrical high tension, as the next line makes clear, for 'flame out' hints at lightning. It is the same metaphor which Hopkins used as an image of God's love in stanza 7 of 'The Wreck of the Deutschland': 'Thence the discharge of it'. And Hopkins's journals show he was a keen observer of this most striking of natural phenomena. The word 'lightning' occurs half a dozen times in his poetry; to him it was a potent proof of God's power, even if that power might be destructive. In choosing such imagery he is also responding, consciously or not, to one of the great intellectual crises of the nineteenth century. For it was the discoveries of the physical and natural sciences which challenged, and sometimes destroyed, the religious faith of countless intelligent Victorians by questioning the Biblical account of creation and promising to offer a rational explanation for what had been thought of as acts of God. By delightedly using imagery of lightning, Hopkins is confronting the doubters head-on, and seeming to insist that the language and discoveries of science can be seen as further proof of God's power rather than an undermining of it.

The two similes which follow have often been misunderstood. By 'shining from shook foil' Hopkins means the thousands of points of light reflected from shaken gold leaf or foil. 'The ooze of oil/

Crushed' is olive oil, for centuries a precious and holy commodity. As often in his poetry, Hopkins is insisting on the opposite, apparently contradictory qualities which are fused together in God: his power is both as sudden as the lightning and as slow as the oil.

Given all this evidence of God's grandeur, the poem says, why do people take no heed of ('not reck') his power ('rod')? Lines four to eight might be read either as the answer to this question or as instances which illustrate how men do indeed not reck his rod. Is it *because* 'all is seared with trade' that people have got adrift from God, or is that searing with trade one instance of their being adrift? We shall see. In writing of 'trade' and 'toil' Hopkins is revealing characteristic late-Victorian attitudes. Around 1830 it had been possible for Thomas Carlyle, one of the most influential nineteenth-century thinkers, to say 'all work is noble, and work alone is noble'. But by Hopkins's time, after fifty more years of rapid industrialisation, people saw that there was a difference, as the socialist aesthete William Morris argued, between useful work and useless toil. Hopkins knew, too, that the word 'trade' is etymologically connected with 'trod', used so effectively in the previous line. He is describing a general weariness, a spiritual affliction, which also has a very material and political aspect.

At the end of the octave, Man has devastated nature ('the soil/ Is bare now') and is cut off from it ('nor can foot feel'). The sestet, as is usual in a sonnet, presents a contrast or a new turn of thought. Despite man's follies, the 'freshness' of nature is 'never spent'. It begins to look as though Hopkins is writing an escapist poem, saying 'Industrial society is an ugly slavery; but fortunately we can turn our backs on it and take refuge and comfort in those parts of nature which remain unspoiled'. In fact this is not the point at all. Nor is this primarily a nature poem. It is concerned with the proper relationship between four things: man, God, man's works, and God's works. They are closely connected, just as the second part of the poem is much more closely connected to the first than it appears to be.

In line 12 we find 'Oh' and in the last line 'ah!'. These are what they appear to be, charmingly straightforward expressions of delight at beauty. Hopkins often exclaims thus in his poetry. But they are also something much more ingenious. 'Oh' is exactly the sound of the letter omega, the last of the Greek alphabet, and 'ah' is alpha, the first letter. And it was Christ who said 'I am Alpha and Omega, the beginning and the ending'. When Hopkins gasps and sighs at the beauty of the world he is also delighting in Christ whom he recognises within those beauties. But there is a further complication. In the alphabet, alpha is first and omega last; in the poem, 'Oh' precedes 'ah!'. Why is Hopkins reversing their natural order? Notice what each is associated with: 'Oh' with 'morning' and 'ah!' with the 'bright wings' of the Holy Ghost. Hopkins is telling us, as one critic has put it, to read nature backwards. 'Morning', the beauty of the sunrise, is what all mortals can see with their own eyes. They should realise that this is merely the end of a chain, its omega. At the beginning of the chain is alpha, the Holy Spirit, the cause of all things, visible and otherwise. So if we read nature properly we see in it evidence of God's presence.

This now causes us to reconsider the first part of the poem with its industrial episode. God is really present in nature, but he is not properly present in people who do not 'reck his rod'. This is why nature is 'never spent' and also why man's works are full of suffering and misery. This poem, then, recognises the existence of social evil, and also proposes a remedy. When man is adrift from God, man's works (the organisation of society) are at odds with God's works (nature) – hence 'the soil/ Is bare now'. Further, man's works are not even adapted to his own well-being. The remedy is to recognise that God should be present in us as much as in nature, that we too are an omega to God's alpha. Only then can the evils described in the octave be put right. The world, then, is seared with trade because people are adrift from God, not the other way round.

'God's Grandeur' is a complex poem which can also be read as a simple praising of God's presence in the world. The intricacies of meaning are there if we want them, but Hopkins would scarcely have objected if readers missed some of them. He was a lover of holy simplicity and straightforwardness as well as of ingenuity and compli-cations. All of these, he would have said, are aspects of God in man.

'The Starlight Night'

The first word of this poem, 'look', is to be repeated six more times as the poet eagerly urges us to use our eyes. Exclamation marks crowd into the text in excitement at the beauty of a starlit night. Every image in the octave describes those thousands of points of light in a dark sky. Clustering together, they look like 'boroughs' or 'citadels', or like winking spots of sunlight in the dimness of woods. The 'gold' on the grey lawns refers to dewdrops catching the dawn sunlight. The whitebeam and the abele (white poplar) are both trees with white undersides to their green leaves, so that they 'flare' with contrasting colours when caught by the wind, just like the whiteness of doves' wings suddenly flashing. These images are from the natural world on earth, but are all being used as metaphors for heaven and the stars. What they all have in common is, firstly, multiplicity (thousands of points of light) and secondly, startling visual contrasts which appear suddenly and unexpectedly. In this way they are very like the image of 'shining from shook foil' in the previous poem, and like the images of the plough and the embers at the end of 'The Windhover'.

Heaven, then (the starlit sky) is like the earth, full of sudden beauty breaking forth. We should now recall stanza 26 of 'The Wreck of the Deutschland', with its similar description of the sky. It went on to say, if the mere *appearance* of heaven to mortal eyes is so beautiful, how much more beautiful must be the spiritual substance, the reality of heaven? 'The Starlight Night' makes the same point in its sestet. All this visible beauty is merely the 'barn', the enclosure or outward structure. What matters is the harvest inside: the 'shocks' are bundles or stooks of corn, though the word also carries its more ordinary meaning: Hopkins once wrote of the few people in history through whom 'human nature saw something, got a shock'. The greatest example of such a person was Christ, the 'spouse' of all mankind, who is shut home in heaven like the corn in the barn. Hopkins imagines the barn as loosely built of wooden slats with the light shining through the gaps ('piece-bright paling'), again a visual analogy with the stars, as if the night sky were a vast sheet of black material with only pinholes to let through a little of heaven's light.

This is why line 8 talks of a 'purchase' and a 'prize': heaven's beauty can be bought, or won, by living a Christian life of 'Prayer, patience, alms, vows'. In a sermon Hopkins once said that Christ's blood 'purchased' the whole world; as a result it is possible for him in turn to purchase Christ.

The poem makes less use than usual of the sonnet's 'turn', for the excited 'looking' of the octave continues in the sestet, suggesting, perhaps, that the beauty of heaven and that of the earth are all of a piece. Two unusual words in the sestet are 'sallows' (willow trees) and 'hallows' (saints). Again as in 'God's Grandeur' Hopkins plays significantly with 'O' and 'Ah' in reverse order: it is worth working out the implications here too.

Like 'God's Grandeur', the poem is in standard rhythm with some 'counterpointed' feet (trochees substituted for iambs). But it exhibits more metrical freedoms than 'God's Grandeur', with some lines verging upon sprung rhythm in order to quicken the pace and convey excitement.

Again like 'God's Grandeur', this is not so much a 'timeless' poem about the unchanging beauties of the universe, but a poem which bears the traces of particular historical and intellectual developments. For some the idea of other worlds in space could pose a challenge to conventional Christian beliefs. But for Hopkins, and for others such as the seventeenth-century French thinker Pascal, the infinity of the universe powerfully suggested the infinite nature of God.

'Spring'

The octave of this poem is Hopkins at his most easily understandable: he is not always a difficult poet, and he had nothing against simplicity. In the sestet, in fact, it turns out that the poem is partly *about* simplicity, the 'innocent mind' of 'girl and boy'.

The charming comparison of speckled thrush's eggs to 'little low heavens' is a link with the previous poem in that it finds images of heaven in miniature on earth.

In the sestet it is Christ who is asked to 'have' and 'get' those innocent minds, to win them over to him before they 'cloud', 'cloy', or 'sour' with sin. It is quite appropriate that this poem should refer to the innocence of children (a characteristic theme of Romantic poetry) because they are metaphorically in the springtime of life and so are a parallel to the literal images of spring in the natural world. Likewise the reference to the Garden of Eden suggests the springtime of the world itself, before sin came into the world with the fall of man. And at the end there are two references to the Virgin Mary: 'Mayday' because May is Mary's month, and 'maid's child' as a way of naming Christ. Again the point is that Mary was free from original sin. So the images of spring, Eden, children, and Mary all work together to suggest that despite the fall of man, Paradise is not entirely lost: it continues to exist on Earth. In the minds of children or the annual rebirth of nature is a glimpse of heaven which all can see, just as in the 'little low heavens' of the thrush's eggs.

'The Lantern out of Doors'

This is another night-piece, but unlike 'The Starlight Night' it is about the human world, not the heavens. Its subject is fellowship and friendship, attraction to and interest in one's fellow human beings. The lantern 'wading' in the sea of darkness 'interests' one's eyes, prompting curiosity about the solitary figure carrying it. In lines four to eight this becomes an image of humanity in general. Exceptional individuals, made 'rare' by beauty either physical or mental and spiritual ('mould or mind'), provide the 'rich beams' of illumination in an otherwise murky world. Light in this metaphorical sense, meaning truth or virtue or beauty, is one of the oldest of poetic images. From undergraduate days onwards Hopkins set a high value on human friendship. Here he laments its unavoidable loss, as one person after another is taken away by 'death or distance'.

The repetition of 'death or distance' at the beginning of the sestet, against the spirit of the sonnet's 'turn', emphasises the note of lament, as if he is dwelling on the fact of separation. 'Wind', to rhyme with 'mind', is a verb; it goes with 'after', as does the verb 'eye'. The meaning is 'however I may follow what most attracts my gaze, I cannot be in at the end'. The strange, straining syntax and word-order here suggests the 'winding', an eager and curious following of something elusive. But it is followed by all-too-familiar phrases: 'be in at the end', 'out of sight is out of mind'. Such proverbial wisdom, though little finer in its language than cliché, has a habit of conveying the blunt and unavoidable truth: here, it is the realisation that in seeking to preserve such friendship he is struggling against the inevitable and the impersonal.

The remedy is in the closing lines. Christ 'minds', and the word means 'takes care of', 'cares about', and 'holds in mind' all at once. In all these senses he 'looks after' those who would otherwise be lost in the darkness. Other words from earlier in the poem now return in pointed new senses. Christ's 'interest' 'eyes' them, his 'heart wants' them, his 'care haunts' them, and so on. At the end of the octave we read that 'death or distance buys' the lost friends. Now, at the end of the sestet, Christ is their 'ransom': he buys them back. And in this series of metaphorical financial transactions, the 'interest' is his. But 'interest', the word first used of the lantern attracting the eye, now also contains an echo of its senses in Latin. There it can mean 'to be between', and also 'to be of concern to'. So this single word now sums up the two main subjects of the poem: the separation of friends, and the fact that Christ is the friend who never lets one out of mind. In the phrase 'first, fast, last' a word becomes its opposite in two easy steps by changing only one sound at a time: given Hopkins's concept of God's nature, opposites are not as far apart as they might seem.

'The Sea and the Skylark'

Walking by the sea (that, as it happens, was the original title of the poem) at the small Welsh holiday town of Rhyl, the poet hears two sounds which have remained, and will remain, unchanged through the ages ('too old to end'). The sounds cut a path into his ears: the word 'trench', related to the French 'tranche', can mean cut or slice. On the right is the sound of the tide, which, in another energetic verb, 'ramps' against the shore. From his left, the landward side, comes the singing of a lark as it soars heavenward.

Having chosen two sounds as his subject, Hopkins takes particular care with the sound-effects of his language. The poem 'was written in my Welsh days, in my salad days', he later explained, 'when I was fascinated with *cynghanedd* or consonant-chime'. He added that in such poetry the sense sometimes gets the worst of it. Not, however, in the first four lines, where the meaning is plain. Notice in those lines the long vowels and diphthongs which echo the slow roar of the tide. Lines six to eight, where the patterning of consonants really gets under way, are more difficult. Hopkins explained their meaning in detail in letters to his friend Bridges, but the best way of understanding them is to compare the final version with this earlier draft:

> With rash-fresh more, repair of skein and score,
> Race wild reel round, crisp coil deal down to floor,
> And spill music till there's none left to spend.

The lark renews ('more, repair' in the draft; 're-winded, new-skeinèd' in the final version) his song over and over again, and each time it is as fresh and impetuous as before. The song is imagined as a musical 'score' written on the sky; as the bird ascends, it unreels itself downwards as rapidly as a rope or fishing-line whirling off a 'wild winch'. 'Skeined' and 'curl' ('coil' in the draft) are alternative metaphors for the unwinding reel of song. This is the kind of ingenious sustained comparison or 'conceit' which often in Hopkins reminds one of seventeenth-century poetry.

As usual in these poems, the octave has concerned itself with brilliantly observing the energy and variety of the natural world. But, instead of drawing out the implications of the octave, the sestet here presents a stark contrast. Sea and skylark deal out their beings as they were created to do, but man, and the world he has made and marred, are not as they should be. Created as the highest of God's creatures, 'life's pride and cared-for crown', man has lost his primal innocence, has broken his 'make', and is on the way to 'dust' and 'slime'.

In the language, too, there is a great contrast between octave and sestet. The particular is replaced by the general. The town is 'shallow and frail', the time 'sordid' and 'turbid'. No doubt they *were*; but we never find out how or why. The poem merely asserts it, rather than demonstrating convincingly in what particular way they were so. Consequently it risks, for a moment, sounding conventional and opinionated. It is the adjectives, not the attitudes, which are the problem, for in other poems Hopkins handles the same theme of fallen man's degeneracy with complete success.

Behind this, however, lies a deeper contrast. Sea and skylark belong to an eternal world, 'too old to end', man to the temporal world. There is no 'time' (line ten) in the first part of the poem, except for the endlessly recurring cycles of moon and tide. Man's consciousness forces him to live in time. If so, he should pay heed to the Christian injunction to think on his mortality, regard his 'end'. 'Dust to dust, ashes to ashes': that is the fate awaiting man's *body*. But the bird, traditional symbol of the *soul*, soars heavenward. What is to be one's fate: dust, slime – or the life to come? This, or something like it, is perhaps the unspoken implication.

'In the Valley of the Elwy'

The valley of the River Elwy, a place of exceptional beauty, joins the larger and more open Vale of Clwyd close to St Beuno's. The beauty of 'this world of Wales' (line ten) has sent the poet's mind back to another blessed place which is described in the first part of the poem. That house, with its kind inhabitants, was, as it happens, far away, near London. Kind in themselves (the word suggests 'belonging to the human species', as when Hamlet puns 'A little more than kin, and less than kind'), they are aided in their good nature by their surroundings. The 'air' is 'cordial', which means 'of the heart', so that nature and man become indistinguishable in their living kindness. Hopkins always took the view that people were much influenced by their environment (hence his horror at the squalor of Liverpool and Glasgow, physical misery which was also destructive to the spirit). Here, nature nourishes the inhabitants as a bird mothers its eggs or frost-free nights protect the buds and shoots ('morsels') of spring. The conversational language of line eight stresses how natural and right it seems for man and his world to be thus in harmony.

The sestet reverts to considering his present situation which had sparked off these memories. Wales is every bit as lovely (not just pretty, but potentially full of love) as that remembered place. But now the analogy breaks down, for here 'the inmate does not correspond', the kindness of the inhabitants does not thrive on their surroundings as it should. As in 'The Sea and the Skylark' we are not told in what way this is so. Theologically, he is on strong ground: according to Christianity, we are all fallen, imperfect beings. But poetically, one might object that occasionally Hopkins falls into the trap of talking about people in very general terms. This is surprising, given his belief that the sign of God's presence in all things is their highly particular individuated essences. According to his own theory, human beings, the summit of creation, ought to occupy a very special place in his poetry.

At least we cannot accuse him of ever despising others. In the second line of the poem he acknowledges that he too was underserving. So at the end he calls on God to redeem those imperfections and failures. The poem is in a mixture of standard and sprung rhythm, which sounds theoretically confusing but works excellently in practice. Both the twelfth and the last line, for example, mix falling rhythms (stress followed by unstress) with rising rhythms (their opposite) to produce a 'rocking' effect. In line twelve that points up the 'swaying' of the 'scales' of justice. And in the last line it brings home the mysterious mixture of opposites which are united in God, his mighty mastery and his tender love.

'The Caged Skylark'

In 'The Sea and the Skylark' the soaring flight of the bird suggested joy and freedom, and hinted symbolically at the ascent of the soul to heaven. Now a similar bird imprisoned in a cage is compared to man's soul, his 'mounting spirit', trapped in the mortal prison of his body, the 'bone-house'. That phrase smells of mortality, with connotations of skeletons and charnel-houses. In such a condition both caged bird and man are less than they ought to be, the bird 'scanted' or deprived, having forgotten the freedom of flight over the 'fells' or uplands, and the man condemned to Adam's curse, the 'drudgery' of work. A day-labourer was one who did heavy manual work for wages by the day. Though the term is centuries old, the day-labourer was vitally necessary in providing the cheap, mobile labour which nineteenth-century capitalism demanded. Even a poem such as this, which is about the human spirit in general, is not exclusively about eternal verities: it also contains particular social and historical meanings.

Lines four to eight are straightforward. Both man and bird have their joyful intervals but also their 'deadly' (death-like) moments of 'fear or rage'. We often speak of being in good spirits or poor. The poem, which is about the spirit and its relation to the body, here makes the point that only in this mortal life is the spirit subject to such reversals and vexation. This, and the word 'deadly' itself, prepare for the sestet, which deals with the new relation between body and spirit after death and resurrection. In that new state, the spirit will not be free of the body, for it will still be 'flesh-bound', but that will be no encumbrance. Only then will it find the 'rest' which it needs as much as the song-fowl returning to its nest. Writing of the resurrection, St Paul said that what is 'sown in weakness' will be 'raised in power': 'there is a natural body, and there is a spiritual body.' As always, Hopkins manages to find an image from the visible world on earth to convey a suggestion of what heaven might be like. In the life to come, body will do spirit no more harm than the rainbow's foot does to the downy flowers which it appears to touch. 'Distressed', as well as its usual meaning, has a hint of the flowers' delicate 'tresses' which a puff of breath would be enough to disperse.

'The Windhover'

More has been written about this poem than about any other by Hopkins. This should daunt nobody: rich and complex though it is, 'The Windhover' does make sense, and does have a graspable meaning.

This morning, says the poet, he caught sight of the minion (in French 'mignon' means 'favourite', 'darling') of morning itself, the 'dauphin' (crown prince) of the kingdom of daylight. Though prince and heir to that kingdom, the falcon is also a king among birds, as it suggested by splitting 'king-dom' across lines one and two. The bird is 'drawn' (both attracted and outlined) by the 'dapple' of the 'dawn'. As he rides the air in masterful flight, is it the bird, or the air underneath him, which is 'rolling', 'level', and 'steady' all at once? Literally it is the air, of course, as that long, rapid adjectival phrase of line three shows; but the bird is so perfectly adapted to the element in which it moves that the distinction between the two is neatly blurred. Hopkins succeeds in inscaping the power, poise, and variety of movement in the bird's flight by crowding verb after verb into the octave – or if not verbs then words which were verbs before he heightened the surprise by turning them into other parts of speech: 'caught', 'riding', 'rolling', 'striding', 'rung', 'wimpling', 'swing', 'sweeps', 'hurl', 'gliding', 'rebuffed', 'stirred', 'achieve'.

By contrast the sestet opens with a cluster of nouns (line nine). They sum up the bird's qualities, and, in fact, stand for all such beauty in the created world. And they lead up to the crucial verb, 'buckle'. The importance consequences of that verb are emphasised by the capitalised 'AND' which follows. It is the whole mortal, visible world which buckles, or collapses, to reveal for a moment a glimpse of the spiritual beauty within, infinitely lovelier and more powerful ('dangerous'). That beauty, as always in these poems, is Christ's: he is the true crown prince, *mignon*, and chevalier, and it is his beauty that the bird echos. If the poet's heart is thus 'stirred' by a bird, how much more by its creator.

The poem ends with two more instances of Hopkins's unmatched ability to find images in the physical world which illustrate spiritual events. Even the 'sheer plod' of dragging a plough is enough to make the newly-opened earth shine in the furrow ('sillion'). The final image is a more elaborate version of the 'fresh-firecoal' of 'Pied Beauty' (see below). Embers on a fire, 'blue-bleak' on the outside, split open when they fall to reveal burning brilliance within. 'No wonder', then, that the far more graceful actions of the living bird suddenly open up a window onto inner beauty too.

The poem is in sprung rhythm. Contrast the rapidity of the lines describing the bird's flight with the hammering stresses of the final line. Rhyme in this poem is even more ingenious than usual. Though the usual scheme of the Italian sonnet is preserved, in the octave the *a*-rhymes (lines 1, 4, 5, 8) are masculine and the *b*-rhymes feminine, yet all eight contrive to end in '-ing'. Further, every *a*-rhyme is a noun and every *b*-rhyme the present participle of a verb. Verbs do and nouns name: here, because of the rhyme-scheme, the actions (of the bird) are tightly intermeshed with the naming (of Christ). These are only a few instances of the ways in which the poem's intricately patterned language heightens its meaning.

Superb poem that it is, 'The Windhover' deserves the attention it has received. Unfortunately it has often received it at the expense of some of the other poems and of the group as a whole. Readers have been attracted to 'The Windhover' for many good reasons, but also for one dubious reason, namely that Hopkins once described it as 'the best thing I ever wrote'. Never mind the question whether poets are the best judges of their own work; the fact is that Hopkins made that remark in June 1879, fully ten years and nearly thirty poems before the end of his career. It was not a final judgment.

'Pied Beauty'

This sonnet is unusual in being 'curtal', curtailed, with six lines instead of eight in the first part and four-and-a-bit instead of six in the second. Hopkins hoped that this arrangement would preserve the proportions of the original on a smaller scale. But this poem, though done in miniature, is full of the essence of Hopkins's beliefs and way of looking at the world. Its unusual form is appropriate, for this will turn out to be a poem about uniqueness.

'Dappled' in the first line is the key to the images which follow, for they all stress visual variety or contrast. 'Brinded' means brindled or streaked. The 'rose-moles', white and pink circular markings, on the trout contrast with the colour of the rest of its body; finches' wings too are many-coloured. 'Fresh-firecoal chestnut-falls' is a highly condensed visual comparison between chestnuts which split open when they fall to reveal the brown nut within the pale green shell, and coals on a fire which likewise burst open, black on the outside but glowing orange-hot within. This is a restatement of the closing image of 'The Windhover': the 'blue-bleak embers' which 'gash gold-vermilion' when they fall. A patchwork landscape also exhibits variety and contrast, with some fields brown from the plough and others, pasture or fallow land, different shades of green. Human beings, too, add to the endless visual variety of the world with all the 'gear and tackle and trim' of different occupations. For all these things, the poem says, 'glory be to God'.

Or rather, it says 'Glory be to God for . . . ' [all manner of things, which are then listed]. Then the second part of the poem begins with 'all things', and ends with 'praise' to God. Thus the two parts of the poem are like mirror-images of each other: God begins and ends the whole poem, while all the things of the world end the first part and begin the second. The word 'all' (significantly, it is the word which Hopkins uses more than any other throughout his poetry) occurs in both lines six and seven. Thus the 'all' of the world is infolded, as it were, within God, who is, as usual, both beginning and end, alpha and omega. The syntax of the poem continues this mirror effect. In the first part, subject, verb, and predicate are in their usual order ('Glory be to God . . . '). But in the second part, what we think at first reading is the subject ('All things counter . . . ' and so on as far as 'adazzle, dim') turns out to be the object of the verb 'fathers-forth'; the subject is 'He'. We are forced to revise our assumption about the grammar of the sentence just as Hopkins is asking us to revise the way we read the world. When we contemplate the infinite variety of the changing world we should take that as proof that it was all created by the one being who is *past* change. When we see and praise beauty in all its variety we should realise that we are in fact praising *him*. In one of the manuscripts of the poem there are stresses marked as follows:

He fathers-forth whose beauty is pást change:
Praise him.

To read it without those two stresses is to miss the point.

As we noted at the end of 'The Wreck of the Deutschland', many a Jesuit would begin a piece of writing with the Jesuit motto, Ad Maiorem Dei Gloriam – to the greater glory of God – and end it with the words Laus Deo Semper – praise to God always. 'Pied Beauty' begins and ends with those same phrases only slightly reworded. In that sense it is, like many a Hopkins poem, a purely traditional piece, a spiritual exercise, a meditation on a set and familiar subject. Such traditionalism does not preclude, rather it offers scope for, high originality. Hopkins chose to work in a briefer than normal form on this occasion, but he had even more to say than usual. 'Pied Beauty' also helps explain why some Hopkins poems have a highly complicated surface and yet a very simple underlying meaning. For him, as the poem shows, the world itself was like that: no wonder that his own poems do likewise.

'Hurrahing in Harvest'

This poem, wrote Hopkins, was 'the outcome of half an hour of extreme enthusiasm as I walked home alone one day from fishing in the Elwy'. The enthusiasm, as so often in Hopkins, is for the beauty of the world and God's presence in it, and it brings the group of sonnets to a triumphant conclusion.

The ecstatic mood is created by sprung rhythm at its most energetic and by exuberant rhymes. It is not only the clouds whose 'behaviour' is 'wilful' and playful: Hopkins's language is too. Note the *b*-rhymes of the octave, 'behaviour', 'wavier', 'Saviour', and finally, overrove across lines eight and nine, 'gave you a/ R . . . '. There are five stresses per line, and the freedom of sprung rhythm is exploited to crowd stresses together emphatically, as in 'héart réars wings bóld', and also to space them out with slack syllabes, producing the rapidity of the last line. Again, delighting in deliberate waywardness, Hopkins wanted to scan the fifth line

I wálk, I líft up, Í lift úp heart, éyes

The strange stressing of the second 'I lift up' works well enough because it is a contrast – almost a correction – to the first, normal version. It suggests a tone of astonished, if somewhat exaggerated, excitement, as if he can scarcely believe his own actions. As a piece of human *speech* it is credible enough, though very unlike the usual decorum of well-behaved lesser poetry. Once, on picking up one of his own poems and reading it after several months, Hopkins wrote 'it struck me aghast with a kind of raw nakedness and unmitigated violence'. But with equal truth he added 'take breath and read it with the ears, as I always wish to be read, and my verse becomes all right'.

'Barbarous', applied to the stooks of corn, suggests their bearded appearance and their outlandishness. Contrary qualities are fused together: the clouds are 'silk-sack', combining the smoothest and roughest of materials, and God's 'world-wielding shoulder' is 'as a stallion stalwart' but also 'very-violet-sweet'. This is the same dual-natured God, powerful but gentle, that we saw in 'The Wreck of the Deutschland'.

The poem succeeds in convincing us that a personal, living God is made manifest in nature because it repeatedly describes nature as animate, alive. The stooks 'rise' as if unaided, the clouds have their 'behaviour' like unpredictable children, and the heavens give a 'greeting' which seems hardly metaphorical at all because it takes the form of real 'replies' in round language. Concrete rather than abstract imagery is one of the secrets of the energy of Hopkins's poetry.

These things, says the poem, were here and only a beholder was lacking; when one is present, the instresses can strike home. In Hopkins's view all things were created to praise and reverence God by their mere existence, but the special privilege of human beings is that they can offer their praise consciously. The literal meaning of the last line is presumably that the heart, like the body, leaps for joy, but the poem puts it better with 'half hurls earth . . . off under his feet'. In nearly hurling the earth off he is imitating God's own 'world-wielding' behaviour at the start of the sestet. Imitation is not only sincere flattery, but also evidence of God in man. This is a more energetic version of that simple but telling conclusion to 'Pied Beauty': 'Praise him'.

Each of the Welsh Sonnets is complete in itself and may be studied in isolation. But once readers have made the effort to understand each poem individually, they should reconsider each in the context of the others. We have no way of knowing what final order Hopkins intended for the Welsh Sonnets, nor even whether he intended them to be considered as a coherent group. The traditional arrangement – and it is not the one given above – is the work of his later editors. As it happens, the arrangement adopted here fits better with what we know about the chronology of the poems' composition than the traditional arrangement does. But the real significance of whatever order we choose to adopt is more than a matter of chronology. The new order was first proposed by the critic Paul Mariani in 1970, and interested readers should consult his book (see the list of further reading).

Hopkins had perfected sprung rhythm many months earlier, when writing 'The Wreck of the Deutschland'. There can be no doubt that he could have written all the poems of 1877 in sprung rhythm had he chosen to. But in fact we find that the ten poems, when re-arranged as above, begin in standard rhythm and progress slowly towards full sprung rhythm, making one small step of technical innovation each time. It is as if Hopkins had set himself the extraordinary aim of transforming the technical resources of the sonnet in the course of one summer and ten short poems. But, rather than risk baffling his potential readers by unleashing sprung rhythm without warning (as he had done in 'The Wreck of the Deutschland'), he allowed us to see the transformation happening before our eyes in easily grasped stages. Whether this really was his intention will probably remain a matter for speculation. What is clear is that each of the ten poems is metrically slightly different from every other (those differences are outlined in full in the notes to most good editions of the poems), and that, depending on the order we adopt, they seem to form a progression. It is certainly worth thinking about each poem not just on its own but also in relation to the others.

5 POEMS 1877–81

The poems discussed in this chapter take us from Hopkins's last months of study at St Beuno's in Wales in 1877 through to 1881. Those four years saw him working in or around Sheffield, London, Oxford, Manchester, Liverpool, and Glasgow. It was the period of his life when changes of situation came most rapidly and when he was most actively engaged with the world, in parish work and preaching. The poems reflect something of that variety, ranging from short and exquisite lyrics such as 'Binsey Poplars' and 'Spring and Fall' to more elaborate pieces. Two poems here, 'Henry Purcell' and 'Felix Randal', are among the most important of Hopkins's limited number of poems about particular human beings.

The first poem in this group, 'As kingfishers catch fire', is very much in the spirit of the Welsh sonnets. Few of the poems which follow, however, show the same unbounded delight and exultation which was often present in that remarkable group of poems from 1877. The beauty of the world still makes its appearance in the poems which follow, but so too do the themes of mortality, sorrow, conflict, and destruction.

'As kingfishers catch fire'

This sonnet is a good introduction to Hopkins's idea of the 'thisness' of things, their individuated essences,and also to the idea of inscape. (These two ideas are not identical: see the sections of this book on Duns Scotus and on inscape.) The brilliant plumage of the kingfisher catches the light and the dragonfly seems to flame because it is their nature to do so; that is what makes them what they are and not something else. To use the verb of line eight, they 'selve'; or, as lines five and six put it, each thing in the world gives forth ('deals out') the being which dwells inside it. Hopkins chooses 'indoors' rather than the plainer 'inside', at the risk of momentarily confusing us, because it is the more concrete word, suggesting that these mysterious

essences have a very tangible physical embodiment. Tangible qualities, too, are what he inscapes in the stones, which, in a phrase that
has been turned into one huge adjective, are 'tumbled over rim in
roundy wells'. The reeling energy of that second line comes from a
clever manipulation of rhythm and metre. The line is iambic, inviting
us to hear in it patterns like this: 'Ăs túm/blĕd ó/vĕr rim/in róun/dy
wélls'. But the words 'tumbled', 'over', and 'roundy' are all natural
trochees, so that we hear an opposite rhythm overlaid upon the
expected one. The ends of the feet split up those three words when
we listen to the iambs, but when we simultaneously hear trochees
those hints of a break in the middle of the words disappear. Our sense
of timing receives a jolt, and the line, like the stones, tumbles and
rings.

It is well worth tracing the pattern of vowels and consonants in
lines three and four. It is also worth considering this earlier version of
line nine:

Then I say more: the just man justices

Many readers would say this is inferior to the line as we now have it.
If so, why?

This poem was probably written at the same time as the Welsh
sonnets, and has much in common with them, including the way in
which the octave deals with the physical world and the sestet with the
spiritual. The verb 'justices' in line nine means 'lives the good, or
just, life'. It is in the just man's nature to do so, as it is in the nature of
the kingfishers and the stones and bells to do what they do. This is
Hopkins's usual view of goodness and virtue: natural, sweet, and
attractive, it is not something that has to be won by an arduous
struggle. Yet it does depend, crucially, on grace, which is an
important word in this poem. Grace is the theological term for the
divine influence which works in human beings to regenerate, sanctify,
and inspire to virtue. In an essay on grace Hopkins once wrote,
almost as if commenting on this poem, that 'grace is any action,
activity, on God's part by which . . . he carries the creature to or
towards *the end of its being*, which is its selfsacrifice to God and its
salvation' (my italics). In being fully themselves, attaining the 'end'
or purpose of their being, even the bells and stones are offering glory
to God. So the loveliness of human eyes or limbs is the loveliness of
Christ within man. The poet takes a fine risk with the threadbare
sentimental word 'lovely', and the risk comes off because the word
suggests 'with (divine) love itself'. Hopkins's essay on grace continues: 'It is as if a man said: That is Christ playing at me and me
playing at Christ, only that it is no play but truth; That is Christ *being
me* and me being Christ.'

58

Written five years after he first read Duns Scotus, this poem shows Hopkins more than ever concerned with the selfhood or particularity of created things. It also shows him quite at ease with the apparent contradiction between this cultivation of individuality and his religious obligation to cultivate self-abnegation. The way he reconciled the two was this: the sheer infinite, ever-changing variety of unique things and beings in the world only went to show, for Hopkins, how they were all created by the being who himself was *not* various nor changeable, that is God. See 'Pied Beauty'.

'Binsey Poplars'

This simple and charming lyric was written out of sadness at the sudden felling of trees in a water-meadow at Oxford. On another similar occasion Hopkins wrote 'The ashtree growing in the corner of the garden was felled . . . there came at that moment a great pang and I wished to die and not to see the inscapes of the world destroyed any more'.

It is in sprung rhythm, and as with 'The Wreck of the Deutschland' the indentation on the page shows the number of stresses to look for per line. Note the heavy, tolling finality of

Áll félled, félled, are áll félled

and contrast the long-drawn-out meandering effect of the line which ends the first stanza. These varying line-lengths, and the irregular rhyme-scheme and stanza-form, suggest a speaker made wilful by sorrow, as the words take up whatever room they need and refuse to be fitted into a regular form.

The leaves of an aspen tree will quiver in the slightest breeze. Hence their visual beauty: the poem says they made 'cages' which trapped, 'quelled or quenched', the sunlight. The word 'folded' in line four continues the idea of an enclosure which contains on the earth the precious light from heaven. Playing through the leaves, 'dandled' like a child on a parent's knee, the light casts shadows which are 'sandalled'. That remarkable adjective suggests the interlacing, and the silent movement, of the light and shade.

In the second stanza Hopkins finds a truly horrifying image to convey his own horror at the trees' cruel destruction: the tender eyeball made useless for ever by a single tiny jab. Despite its shock effect, the image seems to belong in the poem because so much else here is about the beauties perceived by the eyes. One thing which made this 'rural scene' particularly 'sweet' and 'especial' was the encroachment, less than a mile away, of the 'base and brickish skirt' mentioned in 'Duns Scotus's Oxford' (see below). The frequent repetitions of words in this poem are best explained by a comment of

Hopkins's quoted earlier: 'Poetry is in fact speech only employed to carry the inscape of speech for the inscape's sake – and therefore the inscape must be dwelt on . . . repetition, *oftening, over-and-overing, aftering* of the inscape must take place in order to detach it to the mind and in this light poetry is speech which afters and oftens its inscape'.

'Duns Scotus's Oxford'

The opening lines of the poem 'inscape' Oxford, seek out its visual laws, and define its beauty as a relation between things. Those things are the works of man (towers, bells) and the works of God (trees, birds, river). The proper relation between them is one of harmonious co-existence, balance ('coped and poisèd'), and pleasing interpenetration. (This is the very relation which is awry in 'God's Grandeur'.) Even today a remarkable amount of green space, woodland, and water is to be found mixed right in the heart of Oxford. Though we tend to think of such things as 'nature', they are in fact humanly worked: planted, irrigated, diverted, banked, and so forth. In the heart of the town, then, man's works and God's co-operate.

In the heart of Oxford, yes; but not in its nineteenth-century suburbs, hastily erected in raw brick and repetitious architecture in Hopkins's lifetime, and like all new housing unsoftened by trees and plants for the first few years. This is the 'skirt' of line five, surrounding the old city centre, which 'sours' the harmonious relation between town and country in which the city's beauty is 'grounded' (the unnecessary 'which' is omitted both times). One critic has made the fine observation that this poem, written in sprung rhythm, nevertheless contains a single line which is a regular iambic decasyllable in standard rhythm. It is line five. The line which describes an unwelcome encroachment on the city is itself, metrically speaking, an intruder. The 'base and brickish skirt', however, is more than merely unwelcome, and something more fundamental than the fastidious aesthete's dislike of ugliness is at stake here. The new buildings are called 'graceless', a word not to be used lightly (see the discussion of 'As kingfishers catch fire'). The point of this will emerge shortly.

As the sestet begins, the poem seems to 'turn' to something very remote from the octave indeed. Turning its back, as it were, on nineteenth-century Oxford, it appears to draw comfort from the fact that Scotus, Hopkins's favourite philosopher, knew this spot too, even though that was more than five and a half centuries earlier. By the last line the poem has apparently wandered off to France, recalling Scotus's defence in Paris of the doctrine of the Immaculate Conception – 'Mary without spot'. (See the section of this book on

Duns Scotus.) It might seem as if this is an escapist poem, seeking consolation for modern ugliness by dreaming of other times. But in fact this is a poem like 'God's Grandeur': it has a rigorous, taut structure to the thought, but that structure is almost hidden and needs careful exploration.

The first clue is that word 'graceless'. Catholic prayers describe Mary as 'full of grace': here, then, is one link between octave and sestet. Next we need to know that although Scotus propounded the doctrine of the Immaculate Conception in the early years of the fourteenth century, it was not made an article of faith for Catholics until 1854. After many centuries, one aspect of Scotus's teaching finally became acceptable. Now Hopkins wrote the poem in 1879: it marks the 25th anniversary of that acceptance, and celebrates long-neglected wisdom now at last recognised.

But in the closing lines Scotus is praised for another, quite different, aspect of his thought as well. He was the 'unraveller' of 'realty': he insisted that it was possible to know the real world directly through the senses. In this he showed finer insight than the greatest philosophers, whether the ancient Greeks or (perhaps) St Thomas Aquinas, born in Italy and the writer whom many Jesuit theologians followed.

The reader is now left to ponder these juxtaposed images and ideas, to supply the connections and construct them into meaning almost as we have to do with a modernist poem like T.S. Eliot's *The Waste Land*. It took hundreds of years, says the poem, for one aspect of Scotus's thought (the Immaculate Conception) to be widely recognised. Perhaps in time people will learn that he was right about 'realty' too: that by using eyes and ears we can know the things of this world, and know God in them. If so (and here the close link between octave and sestet finally emerges) they would realise that man's works ought to be in harmony with God's works. The ugly buildings violate that relationship, and in doing so violate too the relationship between man and God. Lacking 'grace', the new buildings are unfit for human beings, unsuited for their needs and purposes. Here is one of the ways in which Hopkins's poetry engages directly with contemporary social questions. He cared about every aspect of the way in which people live: in that sense, and it is the most important sense, he is a political poet as well as a poet of the natural world.

'Henry Purcell'

Hopkins was a music-lover all his life and in later years spent much effort in mastering the principles of musical composition. This poem is a tribute to the greatest of seventeenth-century English composers. Writing about the individuality of another's art, Hopkins is himself at his most uncompromisingly individual here, and the poem's difficult syntax forced him to provide much explanation of its meaning in letters to his friend Bridges. These are reprinted in many editions of the poems and should be consulted.

'I hope Purcell is not damned for being a Protestant, because I love his genius.' That, wrote Hopkins to his uncomprehending friend, was the meaning of the first four lines. It is instructive to compare that amusingly blunt prose paraphrase with the poem as we actually have it, and to see what is gained, or lost, by the difficulties of expression.

'Fair fall' in the opening line would mean 'may fair fortune befall'; this is then turned into the past tense, so that 'Have fair fallen' means 'may fair fortune have befallen'. Hopkins thus wishes well to Purcell's 'spirit', which is both his immortal soul and, as becomes clear later, the source of his individual, 'arch-especial' artistic genius. An age has now gone by since he departed from life. Purcell the Protestant was '[en]listed to a heresy'; outwardly, that is a 'sentence' of damnation, which lays him low. But (unlike most of us who wish vainly for what *might* have been) Hopkins's trust in divine mercy enables him to hope for what already *may* have been, God's 'reversal' of that sentence. In the headnote to the poem Purcell's genius is called 'divine': if God has indeed chosen to save him, he would simply have been reclaiming his own.

The next four lines explain what it is about Purcell's music which 'finds' the poet, strikes home to him. It is not his 'mood' nor his 'meaning' nor any of the other emotions which his music evokes. 'Sweet notes not his', the work of any other great composer, might equally well 'nursle' (nourish, foster) such things. Rather it is the way his music recounts his own individuality, the 'forgèd feature', the 'abrupt self' which breaks forth from it. The root of the word 'abrupt' is the Latin verb meaning to break away from: we are reminded of the spiritual 'fire' which suddenly 'breaks' from the windhover. As always when Hopkins praises individuality, he is thinking not of self-made beings who self-indulgently cultivate their own personalities, but of God's presence in his creatures. For several centuries Western civilisation has fostered the myth that the individual is 'author of himself', rather than shaped by the world in which he lives. Hopkins was not deceived; in another playful comment he wrote 'My sonnet means "Purcell's music is none of your d--d subjective rot" (so to speak)'.

Like a piece of music which states a theme and then develops it in variations, the poem's sestet elaborates with virtuosic skill the thought which has already been stated in the octave. While Purcell's airs work their effects, raising passions and quelling them ('lift' and 'lay'), the poet will also pay attention to the distinctive self of the composer revealed in the music. 'Air' in line nine of course means melody, but when placed close to the word 'lift' it hints at a soaring heavenward; and the air is 'of angels', almost divine in beauty. Hopkins is still subtly suggesting Purcell's worthiness for salvation.

By 'sakes' (line ten) Hopkins here meant the distinctive quality of genius. More generally it meant the mark which something makes upon the world, some quality by which we can recognise its presence: compare 'sake' in stanza 22 of 'The Wreck of the Deutschland'.

The rest of the poem compares Purcell's 'thisness' to that of the stormfowl. The bird's 'moonmarks' are, said Hopkins, 'crescent shaped markings on the quill-feathers'. The involved syntax of the last four lines has the effect of delaying the flight of the bird so that it surprises suddenly at the last moment. 'Some great stormfowl' is the subject of the sentence, but the associated verb and object are held over until 'fans fresh our wits with wonder'. Like the composer, the bird thinks only of the business in hand, 'meaning' nothing but 'motion'. But as it unfurls its wings and fans the air it unknowingly gives a glimpse of its plumage, 'thunder-purple' like the beach itself before the storm. That glimpse of a creature 'selving' or 'going itself' (as Hopkins put it in 'As kingfishers catch fire') is like the scattering of a colossal smile. In explaining 'wuthering' as 'a Northcountry word for the noise and rush of wind' Hopkins mentioned Emily Brontë's great novel *Wuthering Heights*. The modern reader cannot overlook the parallel between Purcell's music, Hopkins's own poem, and that novel, all products of strikingly individual imaginations.

'The Candle Indoors'

As he worked on it this poem became in Hopkins's mind a companion to 'The Lantern out of Doors'. Both are poems about his attitudes to his fellow beings and about how his instinctive responses to them need improving in the light of his religion. In the earlier poem he was indoors, fascinated by a moving light outside; now, as he passes by outdoors, he is fascinated by a light within. In the earlier poem his sadness at unavoidable human separations led him to recall that in Christ love and friendship are unending; in this poem his curiosity about whether others are doing their full duty to God leads him to remind himself that his first obligation is to do his own.

The yellow, moist light of the candle gently drives ('puts') back the darkness of the night. Its delicate beams run back and forth between the candle and his eye, as if on tramlines (though amid the complex images of line four 'tram' also suggests finely-woven silk thread). As he plods by he wonders who is within and what they are doing. The fact that he cannot know the answer makes him all the more curious, and all the more eager in his hope that they are busy with some worthy occupation, one which could be said to lead to God's greater glory. That eagerness is well conveyed by line seven, which breaks into rapid sprung rhythm, contrasting with the more regular standard rhythm of the rest of the poem.

In the sestet he rebukes himself. He must 'come indoors', put his own house in order, and tend the light in his own heart, before he is worthy to admonish others to do the same. In lines twelve and thirteen, with a pun on 'beam', he conveys his realisation of what he has been ignoring: in pleasantly musing on the beams of light he has become blind to the beam in his own eye. His looking has really been an overlooking. The image depends on our remembering the Biblical words 'Thou hypocrite, first cast out the beam out of thine own eye; and then thou shalt see clearly to cast out the mote out of thy brother's eye'. What Matthew's Gospel calls the brother is the 'neighbour' of line thirteen, whose faults the poet may be too 'deft' and quick in rebuking. And the hypocrite is the 'liar', the one whose salt has lost its savour ('spendsavour' is coined by analogy with 'spendthrift') and whose awakened conscience now judges him as fit only to be cast out. Such rigorous self-examination was part of Hopkins's temperament, as well as being an obligation enjoined upon him by Ignatius's *Spiritual Exercises*.

'Peace'

A 'curtal' sonnet like 'Pied Beauty', the poem is one in which delicate beauties of sound and rhythm are played off against the theme of restlessness and suffering.

The dove is a traditional symbol of peace, but here Hopkins imagines it as a woodpigeon, a 'shy' bird not easily persuaded to settle. We could undo the inversions of word-order in the opening lines as follows: 'shut shy wings', 'roaming round me', 'be under my boughs'. But the point of those inversions, as of the many repetitions, is to suggest the endless circumspection of the shyly circling bird, the refusal of peace to approach directly. In this poem a single sound can make a world of difference: the difference, for example, between 'poor peace' and 'pure peace', which for all their closeness phonetically, are very opposites in meaning. The sound of speech itself is a contradictory thing here: as always, we must hear, not merely read, a Hopkins poem, and what we hear is a voice whose lulling repetitions evoke peacefulness; but the very fact that the voice continues to call makes for a continued disturbance of peace and silence. Amid these gentle invocations and echoes, peace's absence seems ironic indeed. It is no true peace which is constantly interrupted by 'alarms' and the 'wars' of toil or spiritual struggle. If God insists on stealing ('reaving') his peace, surely he should leave something to replace it. He does; it is called patience (which meant to Hopkins the capacity to undergo further suffering), and in time patience will 'plume' or expand into peace itself. For a further insight into patience and peace, see the later poem 'Patience, hard thing!'

In any case, the poem concludes, true peace means something more than mere rest or idleness. Unlike the wooddove now, peace does not come merely to 'coo' at nothing, however soothingly. The dove, in fact, has been transformed from a symbol of peace into the symbol of the Holy Spirit itself. The last phrase, 'brood and sit', echos Milton's description in the opening lines of *Paradise Lost* of the Holy Spirit, which 'Dove-like sat'st brooding on the vast abyss' at the creation of the world itself. We are also reminded of Hopkins's application of 'broods' to the Holy Spirit at the end of 'God's Grandeur'.

'Felix Randal'

Among the best of the poems which Hopkins wrote about particular individuals, 'Felix Randal' tells of the life and death of a blacksmith ('farrier') who was one of his Liverpool parishioners in 1880. The first and last lines of the octave, with 'O is he dead then?' and 'Ah well, God rest him' catch the accents of natural speech and suggest a spontaneous reaction to the news of death. The intervening lines, with shrewd psychology, suggest how such news instantly triggers the memory into recalling and reviewing the closing months of life. In doing so the mind does not begin at the beginning of events, but starts from the recent past and moves further back in time.

Our first image of the blacksmith is of a man in full strength and vigour, 'big-boned and hardy-handsome'. But a moment later, without even any punctuation to make a pause, he is 'Pining, pining', afflicted by the consuming diseases which had taken root in his flesh. It is a startlingly rapid contrast, a reminder of the uncertainty of existence. In lines six and seven 'anointed' refers to the last sacrament, and 'our sweet reprieve and ransom' to communion. They mended the blacksmith spiritually even as he declined physically. In line eight 'all road' is a North-country expression meaning 'in whatever way'. The 'O' of line one and the 'Ah' of line eight are the most natural of exclamations, but also hint at deeper meaning, for 'O', omega, is placed near to the word 'dead' and 'Ah' to 'God': death may be the end, the omega, of life, but it leads back to the alpha, the beginning of all things in God. (See the commentary on 'God's Grandeur'.) And Hopkins forces the familiar expression 'Ah well' to take on a startlingly literal meaning: if 'Ah' is a natural sigh of regret, 'well' conveys Hopkins's faith that it is indeed well for Felix to be with God. His Christian name, after all, means 'happy'.

Throughout the poem the ideas of strength and weakness, beginnings and endings, recur in different ways. Changes are unforeseen: 'How far from then forethought of' (line twelve). The 'big-boned' man of the poem's opening, whose 'boisterous' and 'powerful' maturity is recalled again at the end, is in line eleven a comfortless, crying child even as he nears the end of life. In such ways the poem plays with the contrasts brought about by time, and ultimately becomes a meditation on mutability. Yet it leaves us at the end not with an image of Randal's decline but with a re-enactment of the magnificent God-given strength of his prime, when he used to 'fettle' (fix up, set in order) the 'sandal' of the mightiest of horses. The unexpected word 'sandal' (meaning horseshoe) suggests perfectly how the powerful animal can nevertheless place its feet with delicacy and silence. Among the many effects of rhythm and alliteration which generate the power of the closing lines, note that characteristic Hopkins device in the words 'great grey dray', where words merge into each other by the altering of one sound at a time, as if the poem were writing itself.

'Spring and Fall'

Grief, and the vanishing beauty of trees, are associated in this exquisite lyric as they were in 'Binsey Poplars'. The name of the child suggests precious beauty, for it comes from the Latin for 'pearl'; in Latin the same word is also a general term of endearment, and the poem turns it into a diminutive, almost a pet name, by placing a stress on the last syllable. Interestingly, 'margaretting' was a word Hopkins coined to refer to a certain kind of beauty in ornament and decoration. Goldengrove, the name he uses for the autumnal wood, carries suggestions of a lost golden world, Paradise before the Fall. The trees are 'unleaving' themselves in autumn – 'fall' in the American sense – but 'unleaving' also hints at a reluctance to depart. Other words later in the poem have equally rich connotations. 'Wanwood', a noun, suggests bloodless pallor ('wan'), which is also the colour of 'meal', corn ground to powder; while 'leafmeal' is an adverb coined by analogy with 'piecemeal'. Death in this poem is a pale thing, the fading-away of the fiery autumn colours of the golden grove.

A child weeping over the death of the leaves is really weeping at death itself, for Death came into the world as one of the consequences of that original Fall. 'Sorrow' (line ten), and the 'blight' of the second-last line, are other names for the same thing. For the time being, 'no matter, child, the name': her young mind with its 'fresh thoughts' knows none of this yet, except intuitively, for her 'ghost' (spirit) has already 'guessed'. Time will pass, though, and then she will know it consciously: the fall away from innocence is re-enacted in each growing child. Her heart will grow older, its emotions grow less simple and direct, till she has not a sigh to spare. Even she must come to grief: this is very much the Romantic poet's view of childhood, as expressed in William Blake's *Songs of Innocence and of Experience*, or in Wordsworth's 'Shades of the prison-house begin to close/ Upon the growing boy'. And so for Hopkins a young child in tears becomes the symbol of the sorrows of all humanity.

'Inversnaid'

At the end of his time in Glasgow in 1881 Hopkins took a brief holiday which included a trip by steamer up Loch Lomond, famous for its beauty. At Inversnaid he found a torrent which falls steeply through rocky wooded country into the loch. The inscapes of flowing water had long fascinated him, and he had sketched effects such as the 'coop' and 'comb' of the first stanza. 'Comb' refers to the ridged, furrowed appearance of water as it descends over a fall; 'coop' suggests a cage, or binding in hoops; and the 'fleece' is the frothy whiteness of the water churned to foam. The verb 'flutes' cleverly suggests both a sound and an appearance, for 'fluted' can mean decorated with channels or grooves. Hopkins ranges widely in his search for words rare and fresh enough to be adequate to these sights. A few are Scots, in tribute to the distinctively Scottish 'wilderness' of the scene: a 'burn' is a stream; 'braes' are slopes, and 'bonny' is pretty ('beadbonny', his compound coinage, refers to the red berries of the rowan tree, a species sometimes called mountain ash, which would have been in full ripeness at the season of his visit). Other words are from different dialects: to 'twindle' is literally to bring forth twins, though there may also be a hint of to 'twind', to twist and turn. 'Degged' means sprinkled with water. Hopkins had a strong interest in the etymologies of words. For every startling use of language in his poetry, he could have quoted a parallel or precedent. He took delight in being traditional and original at the same time.

This poem also reminds us that his ideas of beauty in nature were not confined to the picturesque or the conventionally pretty. The pool of stanza two is 'pitchblack', angry and threatening in its 'fell-frowning'. Such a sight might tempt a despairing person to drowning – though the same words at the end of stanza two could almost as well mean that Despair itself is abolished at such a sight. Certainly Hopkins's own spirits are exalted and revived by such fierce and wild aspects of nature. That is a common strain in Romantic poetry. The close of the poem, with its plea to leave the wilderness alone, suggests a Victorian concern about the encroachments of a rapidly-expanding civilisation, understandable in one who had only just come from many months labouring amid the despairing masses of the industrial cities.

6 SONNETS OF DESOLATION

The Sonnets of Desolation, sometimes called the Terrible Sonnets because of their moments of lacerated emotion, date from Hopkins's Dublin years, probably 1885 and 1886. He said that one of them (we cannot be sure which) was 'written in blood'. Other poems from the same period, such as 'Spelt from Sibyl's Leaves', reflect similar dark moods, and for that reason the six poems dealt with below are not the only ones to which the description 'desolate' might be applied. But other poems again, written somewhat later, are much less grim, for example 'Harry Ploughman'. None of these poems is *simply* versified autobiography. Personal though they undoubtedly are, they also draw their strength from traditional motifs and from the common properties of our language itself. Floating free of their origins, they become for us a pure drama of emotion and will. Our estimate of any poem's value depends on its organisation of langauge and poetic effect, not on its fidelity to an original experience, if only because that original experience is not available for us as a test of the fidelity. As one critic has put it, much of their fascination lies in the near-contradiction between their subject and their language: they often describe a loss of vital spiritual energies, but they do so in language which, far from lacking energy, exhibits a 'Herculean athleticism'.

'Carrion Comfort'

Sprung rhythm puts great stress on the repeated 'not' of the first line, enacting the struggle against despair which must constantly be renewed. Despair means more than great dejection and hopelessness: theologically, it is a mortal sin, the state of mind in which a person wrongly comes to believe that God's mercy is no longer available. Thus, though abandonment to despair would provide the 'comfort' of abandoning the struggle, it would be 'carrion', a feasting on death. Such temptation is to be resisted only by an act of pure will:

'I can'. But that refusal to give in cannot quieten, indeed prolongs, his cries of anguish, which occupy the rest of the octave in a prolonged string of questions. The verbs are 'rock', 'scan', and 'fan', as he asks what is God's purpose in thus tormenting him. Yet even as he cries out against torment, he never doubts God's justice: God rocks him with his mighty 'right foot', and though we may at first read 'right' as the opposite of left we realise that it also means just and proper. Even in describing such moments of stress the poem's intellectual and linguistic wit remains.

The image of God as a terrible storm sent to 'fan . . . me heaped there' is the necessary preparation for the start of the sestet where all the questions are answered. The storm's function is to separate the wheat from the chaff. It is worth noticing that Hopkins's faith and consolation here depend upon that *poetic* metaphor, albeit one from the Bible. Faith, and the linguistic sleight-of-hand which is poetry, are often rather similar things. (For some of Hopkins's contemporaries, poetry itself became a substitute for the religious faith which they had lost.)

In the tenth line the poem reveals the trick which it has played upon the reader. The octave has described the torments in the present tense, but from here on, the verbs shift into the past. What we had taken to be an immediate crisis turns out to have been already overcome. The night, which seemed like a year, of 'darkness' is 'now done', as the last line says. His heart has already regained strength and joy. It even cheers the 'heaven-handling' torments which God subjected him to, and cheers himself for his part in that struggle: since it was God within him, the two are indistinguishable. That sudden shift from present to past, catching the reader unawares, is Hopkins's way of showing how different the same events can appear before, and after, he recognises God in them. Terrible and deeply serious though it is, the poem also has a verbal playfulness about it, even down to the near-pun of its last phrases. The hushed exclamation of horror, '(my God!)', as he recognises just who he has been fighting with, is the same as the plain acknowledgement of the literal truth: it was indeed his God. In more ways than one, this is a poem about the surprise of recognition.

'No worst, there is none'

The poem begins not with 'no worse' (i.e. 'there could be nothing worse than this') but with 'no worst': there is no such thing as worst, for things can always get worse still. One 'pitch' or intensity of grief is only the prelude to a greater. He cries to the Holy Spirit, the comforter, and to the mother of Christ for relief, but finds none. His cries are as long-drawn-out as a herd of beasts straggling interminably homewards. Not only do they stretch out, but they huddle together.

In thus being protracted over time but also crowded together, they are like the sorrowing cries of the mass of humanity throughout time, the 'chief-/woe' and 'world-sorrow' itself. In this way his personal lot recapitulates a universal, 'age-old' fate.

Then suddenly the tormented cries 'lull' and 'leave off'. The furiously-expressed demand for a quick end to suffering had brought about that end. The sheer effort of such suffering makes a sudden end essential: 'force' means 'perforce'. As later lines explain, the human being's small 'durance' (endurance) cannot sustain such intensities for long. The remarkable images of the mountains of the mind likewise suggest a crisis suddenly resolved. When one can cling on to the cliffs no longer the collapse follows, a new disaster but also a necessary relief. Yet after the crisis is past, another kind of slow, long-drawn-out process begins, as the wretch has to 'creep' for shelter and wait for the comfort of sleep or death.

In poems such as this where Hopkins is concerned in part with psychological insight, his particular skill is in showing a characteristic sequence or process of emotions, the ways in which one feeling leads to another through turn and crisis. Hopkins may not have written a great many poems about people, but (as we might expect of a post-Romantic poet) there is usually at least one convincing and credible human being in his poetry: himself.

'To seem the stranger'

This is another poem whose origins are both highly personal and highly literary. The solitariness and exile which it describes are what Hopkins actually experienced in Ireland, but they are also part of a long tradition of Romantic verse on that theme. Not all Romantic poets had shared Wordsworth's view that solitude was a blessed state: for many of them, as for Hopkins here, it was a curse. Living among strangers, his 'lot' or fate is to be considered as a stranger by them. It is that lack of acceptance by others which is the hard thing, and it is the key to what follows. Even his own family, whom he still saw and loved, could not help but regard him as set apart from them by his Catholicism, 'in Christ not near', for they remained Anglicans. Hence Christ, who should be (and is) his source of peace, has also become the cause of his separation from and strife with those dear to him.

The second cause of his isolation is that his 'creating thought' goes unheard, even in England, his beloved country, where he would most value that hearing. None of his best poetry, and very few of his scholarly projects, had ever seen the light of day. This is the point of lines five to seven and also of the sentence 'Only what word . . . hell's spell thwarts' in lines eleven to thirteen. The wisest words that his heart breeds are thwarted by 'dark heaven's baffling ban' or 'hell's spell'. (Compare 'Thou art indeed just, Lord', where he says he is unable to 'breed one work that wakes'.) In general the Sonnets of Desolation employ a much plainer and more straightforward syntax than do some of Hopkins's other poems, and that has the effect of suggesting the simplicity of direct emotion. But in lines eleven to thirteen the knotty word-order perfectly conveys the twisted and inexplicable frustrations which thwart and stifle his speech.

The 'third remove', at the beginning of the sestet, is his being in Ireland. But this is also what he alludes to in the last words of the octave, where he is weary of merely standing idly by in a place where 'wars are rife'. In Ireland he felt at odds with his church and colleagues because of their support for Irish Home Rule. This too was a situation to compel him to stifle his self-expression, for now, two authorities in his life, each claiming rightness, were at odds with each other. His allegiance to his fellow Catholics in Ireland, and his loyalty to England as the ruling power, could not co-exist.

The common factor in all three 'removes', then, is not just isolation, but the failure or impossibility of open speaking. Hopkins was a man who loved to affirm and explain; his nature was open and he had a gift and need for friendship. All his work, too, he felt, was coming to nothing. He is compelled to 'hoard' his words 'unheard', or if they are 'heard' they go 'unheeded'. The effect on him is caught in the poem's last phrase, 'a lonely began', with its deliberate 'wrongness' of grammar as the verb is turned into a noun. Thus the very end of the poem, his last word on the subject, speaks of a failure even to 'begin'. And yet, of course, the mere existence of this eloquent poem contradicts, in part, what he is saying: in writing the poem, if nowhere else, his 'word' is not thwarted. Compare 'To R. B.'.

'I wake and feel the fell of dark'

In composing these poems of spiritual crisis Hopkins no doubt had in mind that his situation was one known to others before him. Ignatius had described desolation in the *Spiritual Exercises*. Mystics had written of the Dark Night of the Soul. One of Hopkins's gifts is his power to give spiritual states a very real and concrete embodiment in his poetry, and here he writes of a dark night which is not only metaphorical but also literal and terrifying. Using the present tense, the poem takes us into the middle of the night itself. Hours of suffering have already been spent: notice how the second 'hours' of line two is lengthened into a two-syllable word, suggesting long duration as well as an anguished tone of voice, and more such hours are to come, as daylight delays its return. In line five he speaks 'with witness'. That means he has good grounds, reliable testimony, for what he says; it means, too, that his wits are only too aware of what is happening. But perhaps it also hints at God, the witness of all his doings. Even in his darkest moments Hopkins's faith never wavers. But that makes it all the more inexplicable to him that God, who hears and witnesses, should not heed his cries.

This sonnet is in standard rhythm, but with occasional telling freedoms similar to those of sprung rhythm: in line seven, for instance, the counterpointed second foot (trochaic instead of iambic) puts unexpected emphasis on the first syllable of 'countless'.

The Post Office still refers to its repositories of undeliverable correspondence as Dead Letter Offices. Hence the force of Hopkins's image comparing his unanswered cries to 'dead letters': God is 'away', and the vagueness of 'away' conveys how hard it is to imagine where he has gone.

If the octave ends on that poignant note of abandonment, the sestet retreats within the self and finds only disgust. The searing, bitter taste of heartburn is caused by the acid from one's own stomach rising in the gullet: 'my taste was me'. The spirit would naturally rise up like 'selfyeast', but is held back by being imprisoned in the 'dull dough' of the flesh. His 'curse' is simply to be made of flesh and blood. Such a mistrust of the body was common enough in Christianity generally and in Victorian England too. Even in the Welsh sonnets, in happier days when he had found it much easier to glory in the physical energy and beauty of living things, Hopkins had written of the 'mounting spirit' imprisoned in the 'bone-house, mean house' of the body ('The Caged Skylark').

The sonnet ends with a glimpse of a hell where the most terrible punishment conceivable is to remain oneself. To that he compares his own situation. This is perhaps the grimmest moment in this group of poems, but even here Hopkins does not lose his sense of proportion, for he is aware that the truly damned are 'worse' than he: his state is only temporary.

'Patience, hard thing!'

The opening lines say not just that it is hard to have patience, but that patience is a hard thing even to pray or ask ('bid') for. This is because the person who asks for patience is asking for further 'war' and 'wounds', for the strength to sustain a prolonging of his burden. Hopkins is aware that 'patience' comes from the Latin verb meaning to endure, suffer, or undergo. Patience is usually thought of as a virtue and suffering as an evil. For Hopkins they are more closely related than that; they are two faces of the same thing. We may be reminded of 'The Wreck of the Deutschland': it is a short step from saying that the endurance of suffering is a virtue to saying that suffering itself can be a fine thing. Whether Hopkins really takes that step is a matter for debate. The deprivations and constraints evoked in line four are the antecedent of 'these' in line five. Either patience takes root and flourishes in the midst of such buffetings as these, or it exists nowhere.

A moment ago patience was the 'hard thing' to ask for. But in lines six to eight, it is the kindliest and most 'natural' thing imaginable, drawing a merciful veil over the memories of failure. Abruptly, Hopkins's outlook has been transformed: a moment more and he is showing a flash of his old delight in nature's beauty, in the 'purple eyes and seas of liquid leaves' (patience is also the name of a plant). 'Seas' of soft and 'liquid' leaves make another complete contrast to the earlier images of hardness, wounds, severity. Again Hopkins is dramatising a spiritual *process*, a *sequence* of emotions: patience, and the will to accept further suffering, may be hard to ask for, but once they are obtained, all the world seems different. The words 'There she basks' suggest the speaker actually looking at a particular plant, and the plant, with its 'purple eyes', seems to look back: for a while he is lost in fascinated contemplation, rapt out of misery.

But not for long. 'We hear our hearts grate on themselves', not only because the pain remains but also, perhaps, because of the very contradictoriness of fluctuating emotions. Certainly lines nine to twelve point up one contradiction: asking for patience is asking for an even more costly ('dearer') bruising, yet that is also the only way to reach relief, by bidding God, source of comfort, to subdue the rebellious will.

'He is patient' in line thirteen scarcely seems a logical answer to the question 'where is he?' in the previous line. Yet it *is* an answer: God's apparent abandonment of his creature to prolonged suffering shows, if nothing else, that God himself has patience in abundance. It fills his 'crisp combs', sweet as stored honey; like God's grace or mercy, it can therefore be obtained by man, obtained in 'those ways we know'. That closing phrase avoids naming those ways explicitly: does that imply they are so arduous that they are best not dwelt on, or so familiar and natural that he needs no reminding of them? Perhaps both: if so, the poem's end reconciles in a single image the two contrasting descriptions of patience given earlier, the 'hard thing' and the 'natural heart's ivy'.

'My own heart'

The strictness of Hopkins's self-discipline and the severity with which he scrutinised and judged himself is evident throughout his poetry as well as his life. Here, for once, he relents, recognising the need to be kinder to himself, and recognising too that if he is the tormented one he is also the tormentor. Yet even in the middle of this introspection he has not entirely put God out of mind, for to be 'kind' and 'charitable' is to imitate the qualities which above all others he associated with Christ. The comfort he needs, however, is not easily had. In his comfortless world it is as hard to find as is daylight for blind eyes, or fresh water for those dying of thirst as they drift upon the ocean. But lines five to eight do more than simply explain why his comfortless state makes it urgent that he should take pity on himself. They are a further instance of the way his 'tormenting mind' finds it so hard to break free of the cycle, for in these lines he is again dwelling on his torments – precisely what he had just told himself he should cease doing. Like the other Sonnets of Desolation, then, the poem enacts the successive stages of a spiritual drama.

So the sestet opens with a new effort to relent, 'call off thoughts', and give comfort a chance to grow. Lines nine and ten, with their brief phrases and pauses, catch the accents of coaxing and persuasion, as if in a kindly and direct address to a friend. Given the necessary 'root-room', comfort and joy will 'size' (grow) again, though only God can foresee just when and how. (The verb 'size' also suggests 'draw sustenence', for it was a university term meaning to obtain one's ration of food and drink on account.) One cannot wring a smile from God: rather it comes unexpectedly, as a patch of sky, hanging between two dark mountains, will suddenly 'pie' or dapple the earth with light.

7 THE SONNET SURPASSED

Between 1885 and 1888 Hopkins's sonnets reached their highest pitch of experimentation and expansion. Each of the four poems discussed here uses a different means of obtaining greater length and weight than the ordinary sonnet form permits.

'Spelt from Sibyl's Leaves'

'The longest sonnet ever made', Hopkins called this poem, and added that it was also 'no doubt the longest making'. (That, however, was said in 1886; the 'Heraclitean Fire' sonnet of 1888 is even longer.) Yet it remains a sonnet of fourteen lines with his usual Italian rhyme-scheme: the exceptional length is achieved by using the freedoms of sprung rhythm and giving each line eight stresses. (In the first line one 'stress' falls upon a pause or silence before the last word.) Within this spacious form the poem develops a richness of verbal suggestion much greater than I have space to discuss in full.

This poem is Hopkins's version of the Day of Judgement, a traditional theme in Christian art. The title prepares us for this: the Sibyl of the ancient world, who wrote her prophecies on leaves which the wind then scattered, was often cited as one of the early witnesses to this most terrible of future events. Likewise the word 'spelt' in the title reminds us that glimpses of the future have to be deciphered and interpreted. Hence the poem begins with a vision or *description* of evening, but goes on to *interpret* that picture as an image for the end of time itself.

Hopkins employs all his poetic resources to suggest the slowness and immensity of the change from day to night. The seven adjectives of the first line all qualify 'evening' of line two, which 'strains' towards night. They suggest an unearthly peace and beauty, a change which is harmonious ('attuneable'). But they also contain threatening hints of what is to come later: evening is 'earthless' not only because it is borne in on the sky but also because it will deprive us of our familiar visible earth. It is 'equal' in that it renders all things the same, as colours and shades of difference disappear. Likewise this is not just another night but 'time's vast . . . night' (line two): Hopkins is already preparing the analogy between darkness and the end of time itself. That universality is stressed again in 'womb-of-all, home-of-all, hearse-of-all': night becomes the condition of being, the element in which we are begotten, live, and die.

The meaning of 'hornlight' and 'hoarlight' in the third line has often been disputed, though the patterning of sounds in the line is of equal or greater importance. Both those nouns, however, are the subjects of the verb 'waste' (line four): they waste away as night draws on, so they cannot be the moon or stars. The last vestiges of daylight, yellow as if seen through the horn of a lantern, wind their way to the west and disappear. Higher in the sky a paler light, 'hoar' like frost, also fades. The stars appear, giving heaven its features in points of fire.

In lines five to seven we see the effect of darkness upon the earth. It puts an end to the 'dapple' of things (compare Hopkins's use of 'dappled' in 'Pied Beauty', and the 'dapple-dawn-drawn falcon' of 'The Windhover'). All things become confused, 'as-/ tray or aswarm', mixed through each other ('throughther'). One 'self' becomes 'steeped and pashed' in another, and the world disappears as if in a huge forgetting ('disremembering') or even a tearing of limb from limb ('dismembering'). This is the death of inscape. And in the inscapes of things Hopkins located all their God-given value and beauty: the tone here is of deep foreboding and regret. These are the implications which the heart rightly points out at the end of the octave: death itself, which awaits every created thing, is now overtly the subject. Night is the commonest of poetic metaphors for death. It is worth noticing how Hopkins has rendered that familiar association wholly convincing in the octave, slowly making the transition from the one idea to the other, and preparing for it as early as the first line by the ominous hints which we noted there.

As the sestet begins, the whole visible world has gone, leaving only the silhouettes of the trees against the sky, and they have taken on a nightmare quality, 'beakleaved' and 'dragonish', for their full roundedness can no longer be seen and they are reduced to twisted lines in one dimension which 'damask' or pattern the sky. After this the poem finally makes the transition from the natural world to the spiritual. Everything that has been said so far is now seen as prophetic of what awaits us too; it is *our* tale and oracle, as shown by the stresses on 'our' both in line eight and in line ten. As always when Hopkins contemplates a fallen world subject to death and decay, he turns to the 'world within', for in his view the remedy must be sought in people's behaviour. In the end that behaviour will be judged by God, and the unavoidable rightness of that is recognised in the words

'let life wind off . . .'. The 'skeined stained veined variety' of life
(again the poem reminds us of the infinite richness of the inscapes of
the world, picking up the images of lines five and six) is to be
unravelled like a ball of wool. The sheep are to be divided from the
goats. His vision of judgement is stark and absolute: 'black, white;
right, wrong'. A world where only 'these two tell' is indeed one to be
'ware' of: the last line envisions a hell of thoughts, where the worst
torment of the damned is self-reproach at having deprived themselves
of God. By themselves, of course, the images of the last line could
equally well apply to the torments of a living soul on earth. This
sonnet's bleak conclusion is so unlike the delight in nature of many
earlier poems that readers have often been tempted to draw parallels
with Hopkins's own life at this stage, and to see the poem as the
natural prelude to the Sonnets of Desolation.

'Tom's Garland'

Of all Hopkins's shorter poems this is perhaps the most difficult to
grasp because of its highly compressed syntax. Certainly his friends
Bridges and Dixon found it so, and after discovering with amusement
that they needed lengthy explanations Hopkins wrote 'It is plain I
must go no farther on this road'. Once understood, however, it is one
of his most powerful poems. Like the 'Heraclitean Fire', it is a
'caudated' sonnet (one having a coda or tail), and its two codas
provide an ideal form for satirical invective. Milton's caudated sonnet
'On the new forcers of conscience under the long parliament'
provided the model for the poem's form, and many of the images
come from an unconscious recollection of Shakespeare's *Coriolanus*,
with its tense political controversies.

Hopkins's own excellent explanations are reprinted in the Oxford
and Penguin editions, and should be read, for the commentary which
follows here does not attempt to duplicate them.

The Tom and Dick of this poem, like the Harry of 'Harry
Ploughman', are seen not as individuals but types: Hopkins's argument is a general one, 'upon the Unemployed' as the sub-title tells us.
Tom and Dick are navvies, the manual labourers who in an earlier
period had built the canals (originally called 'navigations') and the
railways which helped make the industrial revolution possible. The
poem glimpses them at the end of their day's work as they pile up
their pickaxes and contentedly make for home, meal, and bed. With
whimsical humour Hopkins imagines Tom's garland not round his
head but as the steel nails on the soles of his boots; they strike sparks
('rockfire') as he walks. Tom's lot is a low one, but he 'swings' (line
eight) his burden 'lustily' (line five). He is not subject to hunger,
sickness, misery, or anxiety (that is the contents of the long parenthesis from lines five to eight). Hopkins says he himself worries little

about inequality ('lacklevel') in the state ('commonweal') provided all have 'bread'. We should seek no further honour than that which comes from our belonging to the same beloved country. That should apply whether we are among its rulers (the 'lordly head' whom Hopkins shows as aspiring to a crown of 'heaven's lights') or whether like Tom we are the 'mighty foot' of the body politic which 'mammocks' (tears, mangles) the earth.

All those mentioned so far have at least some share in the general wealth and well-being. But in the middle of line twelve the poem turns to the unemployed, dispossessed and excluded from the social contract. They are denied the chance to contribute either their 'mind' or their 'mainstrength' and to be 'sped' on by the rewards for work. In his explanation Hopkins called them 'outcasts': 'they share care with the high and obscurity with the low, but wealth or comfort with neither'.

Hopkins has no qualms about his closing description of the unemployed as brutal and menacing. Unusually for a man of such Christian charity, he uses images which turn his fellow human beings into subhuman beasts: 'Hangdog', 'Manwolf'. Such attitudes may appear to owe more to the ordinary social prejudices of the period than to any independent insight or careful thought. Yet on one point the poem is very clear: such brutality is not born but made; it is 'bred' by 'Despair'; and it is the work of fellow-humans, not God. It is the inevitable result of excluding the unemployed from the 'commonweal', turning them into outcasts, and depriving them of 'bread', of the ordinary necessities and decencies of life.

We cannot call Hopkins a great or original political thinker. Equally, though, we should recognise that he was not one of those who thought that religion had nothing to do with political and social questions. He had the courage to judge the way we have organised our world by the light of his Christian convictions. His first-hand experience of the poverty and misery of Liverpool and Glasgow taught him that we have made an unforgivable mess of it. In 'God's Grandeur', another poem with a political dimension, he expressed views consistent with those of 'Tom's Garland': only when the world which we make is fully adapted to our needs and uses, and fully in harmony with the natural world which God has made, will we cease to damage the human spirit.

'Harry Ploughman'

'I want Harry Ploughman to be a vivid figure before the mind's eye; if he is not that the sonnet fails', wrote Hopkins. It is written in 'very heavily loaded sprung rhythm', he said, which is 'altogether for recital, not for perusal'. He added that 'the difficulties are of syntax no doubt'.

Though this is still recognisable as a sonnet, Hopkins has extended the space available by introducing shorter 'burden lines' which, like the refrains of a song, make for a pause and a recapitulation every now and then, though they also add new details.

The 'broth of goldish flue' is the downy hair of his arms, 'breathed' round them as light as air. 'Knee-nave' is knee-cap, and the construction 'onewhere . . . onewhere' in line seven means 'in one place . . . and in another'. In the opening lines all the parts of the body are united as 'one crew' which is 'steered' by the careful 'eye's heed'. All parts are poised for action ('stand at stress'), but as yet they are motionless, though there are so many active verbs used to describe the sculptured shapes of the body ('sucked', 'sank', 'soared') that Harry seems energetic even when at rest and this state of waiting is not very clear. It becomes apparent, however, when we unravel the syntax of the second sentence of the octave: the structure is as follows: 'Each limb's barrowy brawn . . . finds his . . . rank' (that is, takes up its proper position) and then 'features' the deeds which are to come. 'Features' is a verb (its alliteration with 'finds' helps us grasp that) suggesting a figuring-forth of feats. The way in which his limbs all work together as 'one crew' and wait obediently for action suggests their harmonious order, and as they 'stand at stress' we glimpse the tension of the instress which holds this inscape together.

In the sestet Harry moves into action. The easy fluidity of motion is conveyed by the 'liquid' waist and the 'wallowing' of the plough. The wind blows through the curls and locks of his hair: in the bold phrase 'wind- lilylocks -laced' we see their mixing and disorder. In the closing lines his feet, encased in the 'bluff hide' of his boots, race along the furrows while the iron plough beneath throws out a fountain of cold earth in 'furls'.

Despite the highly particular and energetic descriptive language of the poem, Harry is not really seen as an individual but as the very type or essence of any ploughman. The emphasis throughout is on his physical strength, and much of the sonnet is a rollcall (the poem's word) of parts of the body, reminding us that the Victorians were less embarrassed by the admiration of male physique than we tend to be now.

'That Nature is a Heraclitean Fire and of the comfort of the Resurrection'

The ancient Greek philosopher Heraclitus believed that fire, and the constantly-changing flux which it symbolised, was the key principle of the universe. That idea of flux, change and endless variety, was quite in keeping with Hopkins's view of nature. Here the octave re-creates all his old delight in startling visual beauty. Two lines on the antics of wind-tossed clouds are followed by two on the play of light which zigzags and splinters on white walls or is caged and tangled into shadows by the canopy of a tree. The wind beats the earth, drying into dust the mud and puddled ruts left by the earlier rainstorm, smoothing away the footprints and smudges left by man's toil.

Such, then, is the flux of nature, blotting out man's marks – and man himself. If the 'million-fuelèd' fire is the symbol for that ever-changing process, the other three elements of ancient Greek thought (earth, air, water) are also in the poem. But they are arranged in a kind of descending order: beginning with the 'air' of the heavens, the poem plunges downwards, as does the light in line three, and soon arrives at the mire of the human world. The energy of nature is almost man's enemy now, for just as the wind in line five 'beats earth bare' of marks, so in line sixteen 'time beats level' man himself and all his traces on mind and matter.

By now Hopkins has already used up the permitted space of the sonnet, like someone with too many urgent things to say. The poem passes straight on beyond what should be its conventional end at line fourteen, without even having reached its 'turn' which comes with the dramatic cry of 'Enough!' in the middle of line sixteen. In three codas of three lines each the poem goes on to recall the comfort of the Resurrection, the promised transformation of weak, mortal man into the 'immortal diamond' of eternal life. Perhaps it is significant that at the moment when a conventional sonnet would end, this poem is dealing with man's own end; that its 'turn', which is a turn to thinking of Christ's promise, comes very late, in the nick of time as it were; and that its codas, tacked on like after-thoughts, deal with the most literal and important of 'after-thoughts', the thoughts of the life to come. In this way the very form of the poem seems to be a paradigm of the process of redemption through faith.

Though written within a year of his death, this poem shows Hopkins still capable of all his old delight in the infinite variety of nature's inscapes and visual effects. We must always be wary of using poems as if they provided direct biographical evidence about a poet's state of mind. Hopkins's highly-wrought poems are at least as much *things made* as *things said*; they are art as game, not just art as expression. Still, we may draw a contrast between the 'Heraclitean Fire' and earlier poems about the boisterous energies of nature. In the Welsh Sonnets, for example, Hopkins presented those energies as showing forth God's presence; his delight in nature and his certainty about God were all of a piece, and each reinforced the other. But now, he turns abruptly away from nature to thoughts of the resurrection, almost as if they had little to do with each other. His faith does not waver, but joy in nature, one of its old supports, has become an equivocal thing. For nature's perpetual renewal is now apt to make an ironic contrast with his own state of 'joyless days, dejection'.

8 LAST POEMS

In the closing months of his life Hopkins wrote several sonnets in which anguish or dejection are combined with extraordinary linguistic wit, energy, and economy of expression. Clearly his poetic skills and techniques were still evolving at the very end of his career. Yet in these poems he abandons many of the experimental techniques which he had earlier devised for extending the scope and power of the sonnet. This raises a question: if he can now make the conventional sonnet form, with all its resources of meaning acquired over centuries, do what he wants, how necessary were his earlier experiments, innovations, and expansions of the sonnet form? One answer might be that his last poems have more in common with the experimental sonnets than might at first appear. He is still stretching poetic form to its limits. To take one instance, many of the emotional effects in the last poems are generated (as always) by rhythm and metre. The rhythm and metre of the last poems is not actually 'sprung'. But we shall see that many of the effects which follow could have been achieved only by one who had long since mastered sprung rhythm proper.

'Thou art indeed just, Lord'

This is a poem of dejection and frustration written three months before death. The first few lines are a versified translation of a passage from the book of Jeremiah, chapter xii, verse 1, in which Jeremiah complains to God of the hardness of his lot. Hopkins's words mean '[I know that] you are just, Lord, [even] if I argue with you; but, equally, what I plead is just'. The rhythm of the following lines is extraordinarily emphatic:

> Why do sinners' ways prosper? and why must
> Disappointment all I endeavour end?

The metre of this poem – its regular, expected pattern – is iambic. But at the start of both these lines the rhythm – the actual stress pattern as we read it – is trochaic. So we hear the exact opposite of what our ears were expecting, and this gives the words far more emphasis than they could ever have in prose. This is the effect which Hopkins called 'counterpoint'. It is available to any poet writing in standard rhythm, but few have ever carried it so far as this, for there are two trochaic feet in 'Why do sinners' and no fewer than three in 'Disappointment all I'. To write three trochaic feet out of five is to risk destroying our sense of the supposedly iambic metre of the whole poem. Verse form is being pushed to its limits. As so often in poetry, the point of such technical devices is to convey an emotion or tone of voice. Here it suggests anguish, impassioned and impatient speech, and a speaker who is pushing against the constraints of the verse form as hard as he is struggling to reconcile himself to the ways of God. This appears to be the passionate expression of highly personal feelings. And so it is. Yet it is also the rewording of a familiar Biblical text. The personal and the impersonal, or the new and the traditional, are not necessarily opposites in Hopkins's poetry: the one can find expression through the other.

Raging against his lot must not be confused with doubting God's justice or mercy. The poem admitted that justice in the first line, and acknowledges God's love in line 5 ('my friend'). It is *because* he trusts and believes in God so firmly that it is so hard to understand the reasons why he should suffer, while the 'sinners' and the 'sots' and those held in thrall by lust should thrive. Now comes one of Hopkins's most effective touches. An Italian sonnet is divided between lines eight and nine. At the 'turn' we expect a pause, a silence, before the sestet takes a new direction. Instead this powm runs straight on across the turn: ' . . . more thrive than I that spend,/ Sir, life upon thy cause'. Again an expectation about poetic form has been violated. The effect is to suggest a speaker who refuses to be silent at the appropriate moment, whose complaints still ring forth even when he knows he ought not to be speaking.

The images which follow are of the rebirth of nature in springtime. 'Fretty' refers to the finely serrated, or fretted, leaves of the chervil plant, but it also perhaps suggests 'fretting' in the sense of restless sorrowing, as the poet himself is. The main point, however, is that the natural world, though delightful in itself, makes a poignant contrast with the state of the poet, whose works come to nothing. The startlingly powerful phrase 'time's eunuch' is one which is paralleled in a letter written a few months earlier: 'Nothing comes: I am a eunuch', he wrote. Yet he added a crucial qualification: 'but it is for the kingdom of heaven's sake'.

82

'The Shepherd's brow'

Even as an undergraduate Hopkins had often been struck by what he called 'the triviality of this life': it was one of his reasons for believing in eternity, for to him it would be 'incredible and intolerable' if there was no life after death to 'correct and avenge' that triviality. To the Christian all earthly activity and striving is 'vain', empty, compared to the life which is to come. This poem embodies convictions such as those.

For Hopkins lightning was always one of the most impressive manifestations of God's power. Witnessing it, the shepherd is forced to 'own' (acknowledge) something awesome indeed, something for which the strongest descriptive language ('horror', 'havoc', 'glory') is quite appropriate. Likewise the story of the fallen angels, cast out of heaven for their rebellion against God, is a momentous one: their sufferings can properly be called 'majestical' and 'giant'; theirs is a subject fit for tragedy. In such heavenly realms, things of real significance can be said to take place.

In contrast with such things, human life on earth can only seem trivial and diminished. We are imprisoned in the 'scaffold' of bones which is the body; every breath we draw is a reminder of our mortality (*memento mori*). Our lot seems ignominious, not in the least tragic or grand. Hopkins is meditating here upon the fall of man, which, as Milton put it, 'brought death into the world, and all our woe'.

The poem's view of the weaknesses and imperfections of this mortal state is not unusual in Christianity. Lines ten and eleven contain another traditional idea, that earthly fame or distinction is a mere bubble which can do nothing to free a person from the universal limitations of human nature. But, familiar though they are, these ideas are expressed with all the intensity of language which Hopkins once reserved for the expression of joy and delight in the world. The result is a poem which has struck some readers as unnecessarily bitter, even cynical. What it does *not* contain, however, is any suggestion that he feels himself contemptuously superior to his fellow beings. For in the closing lines he too is a victim of the vanity of human wishes, fussily raging at nothing, and mocked by his own distorted reflection in the mirror-like bowl of a spoon. vanity in that sense – self-regard, or pride in one's appearance – is often coupled in English poetry with vanity in the larger metaphysical sense – the emptiness of all earthly ambition and striving.

'To R. B.'

This is Hopkins's last poem, written in April 1889, about six weeks before his death. Appropriately, it is to Robert Bridges, his friend since undergraduate days, and the man to whom we owe the preservation of Hopkins's poetry (see the section of this book on the reception of the poetry).

Most Victorian poets retain the inheritance of Romanticism in their work, and Hopkins is no exception. In the first line it is the 'fine delight' that 'fathers thought'. Part of the essence of Romanticism was the belief that right feeling precedes and generates right thinking, not the other way round; that we can trust what Keats called 'the holiness of the heart's affections' more than the operations of the intellect. Hopkins shares that view here. He is indeed a post-Romantic poet. Living when he did, he could scarcely have been otherwise. But there is no incompatibility between that and his toughly intellectual turn of mind. The particular 'delight' in question is that of poetic inspiration. Like a spur or a blowpipe flame, it touches the mind once, only for an instant, and then is gone. In doing so it 'father' the poem ('immortal song') which then slowly takes shape in the 'mother', the mind. Across the break between lines one and two Hopkins manages to achieve three powerful stresses uninterrupted by slack syllables in the words 'strong/ Spur, live'. This is an effect which we associate with sprung rhythm, but by now Hopkins is able to achieve it within the framework of standard rhythm, so that is power to surprise becomes all the greater. The 'she' of lines 5 to 8 is the 'mother', the mind, which nurtures the growth of the poem towards its birth over a period much monger than that of human gestation ('Nine months . . . nay years'). Though the 'insight' (the delight, spur, or inspiration) is now lost, the widowed mind lives on with a sure purpose. In such poems about poetic inspiration it is traditional to conceive of the relationship between poet and Muse as if they were lovers: hence the imagery of sexual generation here ('fathers', 'mothers', 'nine months'), used as a metaphor for poetic creation.

Not only is this a Muse poem; it is also what we may call a dejection ode. In 'Dejection: an Ode' Samuel Taylor Coleridge had lamented how poetic inspiration had deserted him, and there are many other examples of such poems. So in the sestet Hopkins laments his 'want' (lack) of the 'rapture of an inspiration', and offers with sighs an 'explanation' as to why his 'lagging lines' no longer contain the excitement of inspired verse.

Yet the very nature of a dejection ode contains a paradox. The poet laments his loss of powerful speech, but he does so in speech which is itself powerful. The fact that the poem exists at all contradicts the poet's assertion that he can no longer write. For all its seriousness and pathos, then, this is also a fictional, playful, and self-aware poem. It is full of verbal wit (meaning not humour, but ingenious linguistic play of a kind which reveals unsuspected connections between things). For example, an inspiration is literally a breathing-in, and the poem twice use the word 'breathes'. Close to death, weakened by long years of illness, Hopkins can say with truth that his is a 'winter world' and hint, perhaps, that he too 'scarely breathes' in a literal sense. But in terms of inspiration, he 'breathes' as strongly as ever. And he plays too on 'sighs'. Sighs of dejection are in one sense the opposite of the delights of inspiration. But sighs are also a breathing-out, and therefore the necessary giving-forth of the 'inspiration', the breathing-in. An 'explanation' is literally an unfolding, and so a setting-forth. Words are being used in their radical, or root, senses, to show the deeper connections between apparent opposites.

All these paradoxes are focused in the twelfth line of the poem. What Bridges may miss, what his poems may lack, says Hopkins, is

The roll, the rise, the carol, the creation

Power ('roll'), mounting excitement ('rise'), musical words ('carol') – the words are a perfect embodiment of those very qualities which he claims are now absent from his verse. The line generates an extraordinarily strong impression of *lift*, partly because the nouns become longer and more rapid towards the end, but above all because of the careful arrangement of the vowel sounds. All the vowels in English can be arranged on a scale from high to low: it is because of this that we know, without being told, that 'plink' suggests a higher musical note than 'plunk', or that if two stones are thrown into water, 'splish' is the sound of the smaller stone and 'splosh' of the larger. In this line the vowels tend to rise on the scale as the line goes on, culminating in the 'ee' sound in 'creation', the highest vowel in the language. The contrast between this line and the closing line of the poem could not be greater. Soaring poetic power gives way to short, halting phrases, as if the 'sighs' themselves were punctuating the last line. Hopkins deliberately ends on a flat-sounding word, 'explanation'. In the last months of his life, such dejection was real enough. Yet in his poetry, it co-exists to the very end with a delight in the power of language.

9 CRITICAL RECEPTION

Hopkins died in 1889. Yet with only minor exceptions, his poetry remained unpublished until 1918. Though not entirely averse to the idea of publication, he could not find it in his conscience to take any steps which might promote his own fame as a poet. He could happily advise his friends to publish and try to be known, not for fame but for the good the work might do. But his own first duty was that of a priest. 'If we care for fine verses how much more for a noble life.' He contented himself with an audience of two or three friends. Though his own brilliant and witty letters are full of the most acute literary criticism, he once said that Christ was the only true literary critic and the only one who mattered. He did not even keep a complete collection of fair copies of his own poems. He did, however, help his friend Robert Bridges to do so.

Bridges became the keeper of Hopkins's poetry, and carried out the task with care. But, anxious that his friend's poetry should not be rejected or even ridiculed for its unconventionality, Bridges acted with caution. He introduced a few of the easier poems into anthologies, but delayed the publication of a proper edition until nearly thirty years after Hopkins's death. By 1918 Bridges' own poetic reputation was established, and he had been Poet Laureate for five years. At last he decided the time was right to introduce Hopkins's poetry to the world. But even then he felt obliged to try to forestall hostile responses by including in his edition some harsh criticisms of his own. He talked of faults of taste, occasional affectation, oddity and obscurity, ambiguities, and of Hopkins's attempts 'to force emotion into theological or sectarian channels'.

As it turned out the poems met with more indifference than hostility. It took the Oxford University Press ten years to sell the 750 copies of the first edition of 1918. Not until the second edition of 1930 did Hopkins's poetry begin to reach a wide audience. But from then on, his reputation grew rapidly. The second edition of the poetry could scarcely have come at a more favourable time. The late 1920s and 1930s saw the rise in Britain and the United States of the so-called New Criticism, which revolutionised the reading of poetry. English literature itself was still relatively new as a widespread subject of academic study, and the need was to construct – almost to invent – a literary tradition by declaring some writers to be 'literature' and others not. Because the New Criticism was reacting against what it saw as the amateurish dilettante chattiness of the previous generation of literary critics, one of its criteria for 'literature' was writing which would respond to its new tool of 'close reading'. In poetry, the New Critics valued strenuous, hard-working language which was densely packed with meaning. These qualities, of course, are exactly what Hopkins's poetry offers. They constitute *one* kind of literary excellence; but in the decades when the New Criticism held sway they were often taken to be the highest, or even the only, kind of excellence. Hopkins, then, was quickly appropriated by the New Critics, and used as an ally in their war upon what they saw as the empty and mellifluous sonorities of some late Victorian and Georgian verse. From this point of view even the oddities of Hopkins's poetry, which they interpreted as a refusal to be smooth and easy, were seen as automatic merits. The very same qualities – of 'ambiguity' and 'difficulty' – which Bridges had deplored now came in for high praise. It is certainly true that many of the excellences of his poetry are inseparable from its 'difficulty'. But this book has also tried to suggest, as a corrective to New Critical assumptions which are still widespread, that Hopkins loved simplicity and directness too.

In an essay published in 1932 the influential critic F. R. Leavis outlined the elements of a view of Hopkins which has been current ever since. He argued for Hopkins's uncompromising originality, claimed that the difficulty of his poetry was part of its essence, and that his imagery and the movement of his language could justly be compared with Shakespeare's. He insisted that Hopkins's technical devices are not 'mere musical effects' but ways of 'expressing complexities of feeling, the movement of consciousness, difficult and urgent states of mind.' At the end of the 1920s the full impact of the Great War was still being absorbed and understood. There lay ahead another decade of economic depression and division leading to another global war. The old stable Victorian certainties about the world – and the self – had been discarded for ever. Hopkins seemed relevant to all this too: as Leavis put it:

A technique so much concerned with inner division, friction, and psychological complexities in general has a special bearing on the problems of contemporary poetry.

By 1944, the centenary of his birth, Hopkins was being celebrated as if he were a contemporary figure. This had the somewhat misleading effect of obscuring the ways in which he really was a Victorian, a man of his own period. But the intense interest in his work did at least ensure him serious critical and scholarly attention.

Hopkins's reputation has outlasted the critical movement which first established it, and has continued to grow. Dozens of books devoted to the poetry have now been written; a few of the best are listed in the section on further reading.

In *The Disappearance of God* (1963), a major study of five nineteenth-century writers, the American critic J. Hillis Miller argued that Hopkins's later poetry, such as the Sonnets of Desolation, offers a vision of the self abandoned by God, a vision which is comparable to the crisis of religious faith undergone by many another Victorian. It is not, of course, that Hopkins's own faith ever wavered: in fact, his feeling of abandonment was all the more terrible and inexplicable precisely because he continued to have faith in God. Hillis Miller usefully reminds us that Hopkins's sense of the (temporary) disappearance of God places him with the other Victorians and not in some timeless limbo. We might add that even in his earlier poetry, where Hopkins is constantly and delightedly finding abundant evidence of God's presence wherever he looks, he perhaps feels impelled to keep discovering more and more evidence just because he lived at a time when others were doubting whether that evidence existed.

A few modern readers remain unconvinced. One, herself a distinguished writer, has talked of 'the poetry of a mental cripple'. Such a remark, ludicrous if taken to apply to Hopkins's intelligence, inventiveness, or linguistic control, is really a re-statement of Bridges' criticism about 'emotion forced into theological . . .channels'. These are the criticisms of those who cannot sympathise, even by an act of imagination, with Hopkins's religion, and who vainly wish that we could somehow have had the poetry without the beliefs that sustain it.

A more penetrating modern criticism is that Hopkins, like others in the tradition of the Victorian art critic John Ruskin who valued close and detailed attention to the visible world, was very wise about clouds and sea and trees but not so wise about human beings. If this were so, it would be a serious weakness in his poetry, because he was committed to seeing human beings as the highest and most valuable part of the creation, and he would therefore be weak exactly where he ought to be strongest. For one response to this criticism, see the concluding comments earlier in this book on 'No worst, there is none'.

A poet who perfects an idiosyncratic, highly identifiable style renders it in some sense unusable to later writers even while it fascinates them, for if they adopt it they are condemned to sound like mere imitators or would-be parodists. Hopkins's influence on poetry is not to be measured by searching for the occasional poet who has adopted sprung rhythm or copied his way with a compound adjective. As he himself once said, 'the effect of studying masterpieces is to make me admire and do otherwise'. But in a more general and more important way, his influence on twentieth-century poetry has been profound. Any poet, or reader, who cares for energetic, passionate, highly-organised language is likely to be an admirer of Hopkins. One of the finest living poets, Seamus Heaney, is also a fine critic of Hopkins. To Heaney, Hopkins's words are 'athletic, capable, displaying the muscle of sense'; they are 'crafted together more than they are coaxed out of one another'. Heaney continues:

> It is the way words strike off one another, the way they are drilled, marched, and countermarched, rather than the way they philander and linger among themselves, that constitutes his proper music.

Heaney rightly reminds us that Hopkins's poems are not just *things said* but *things made*. In Hopkins, the power of language is all.

ANALYSIS OF A SPECIMEN POEM

'In honour of
St. Alphonsus Rodriguez
Laybrother of the Society of Jesus'

Honour is flashed off exploit, so we say;
And those strokes once that gashed flesh or galled shield
Should tongue that time now, trumpet now that field,
And, on the fighter, forge his glorious day.
On Christ they do and on the martyr may;
But be the war within, the brand we wield
Unseen, the heroic breast not outward-steeled,
Earth hears no hurtle then from fiercest fray.
Yet God (that hews mountain and continent,
Earth, all, out; who, with trickling increment,
Veins violets and tall trees makes more and more)
Could crowd career with conquest while there went
Those years and years by of world without event
That in Majorca Alfonso watched the door.

As the poem's title tells us, Alphonsus Rodriguez was a laybrother, that is, a member of the Society of Jesus but one who was not a candidate for the priesthood. Laybrothers were employed at domestic tasks. Alphonsus, who died in 1617, was for forty years hall-porter at the Jesuit College in Palma, Majorca. But this outwardly uneventful and peaceful life belied an inner turmoil: in his writings Alphonsus described his fierce and prolonged spiritual struggles against temptation. As Hopkins remarked, 'he was, it is believed, much favoured by God with heavenly lights and much persecuted by evil spirits'.

A reader confronting this poem for the first time could not be expected to know precise biographical details about Alphonsus. This need not be a problem: the poem itself contains enough clues to make an intelligent reading possible. What *is* essential to an understanding of the poem is some knowledge of Hopkins the Jesuit and of the importance he attached to the spiritual life. Equally vital equipment for any reader of Hopkins is a complete familiarity with the sonnet form and its technical resources.

We may begin by trying to grasp the bare outlines of the poem's thought-structure. Honour is 'flashed off' exploit in the sense of being reflected from it. By 'exploit' Hopkins means physical struggle or suffering as undergone by the soldier (lines two to four) but also by Christ or a religious martyr (line five). It is physical heroism of this kind which confers honour – or 'so we say' (line one). Yet in so saying we are wrong, as the rest of the poem implies. For a 'war within', a mental or spiritual struggle, may also be 'heroic' (line seven) and equally desperate (line eight calls it a 'fiercest fray'), but in this case there is no 'hurtle', no outward and visible sign. In this way the poem asks us to redefine our notion of heroism: not to deny it to those who suffer physically, but to extend it to include inward fighters too. Hopkins argues for this redefinition by *poetic* means, showing us unsuspected connections between the apparent opposites of outward and inward strife. Thus Alfonso's purely spiritual career is crowded with 'conquest', a term with connotations of martial achievement. And the references to Christ's (physical) agonies, and those of the martyrs whose deaths emulate his, remind us that to undergo physical suffering may demand great *spiritual* strength.

In the parenthesis from lines nine to eleven we find Hopkins's familiar stress on the dual nature of God, both powerful and gentle. 'Hews' is a very active verb to apply to the (mostly slow) processes by which geological change shapes 'mountain and continent'. Taken in the aggregate, of course, such changes are cataclysmic; and so Hopkins contrasts them with the infinitesimal and delicate processes of growth seen in the violets and the trees. This parenthesis is not just an aside, not a piece of description superfluous to the story of Alfonso: Hopkins is saying that we have the evidence of our senses for a God who is a fusion of opposites, and therefore that we should be ready to accept that other apparent opposites can coexist: that heroism can consist in inner victories as well as physical suffering, or that outward peace can conceal inward struggle. Seeing God rightly, and properly estimating one such as Alfonso, are therefore two aspects of the same enterprise: the achievement of clear sight, the ridding ourselves of customary assumptions (as in the 'so we say' of line one). For in the images of line nine Hopkins is reclaiming geology for God. Long before Darwinism it was geology which had posed the first great challenge to nineteenth-century Christian faith. The evidence of the rocks showed that the world was millions of years older than a literal interpretation of the Bible would suggest. And it showed too, in fossils, that whole species had disappeared, which for some cast doubt on the benevolence of providence and on the assumption that humankind was the ultimate of creation, for humans too might eventually disappear. But Hopkins rejected such interpretations. As with the metaphors of lightning which he often uses elsewhere, he is here implying that the discoveries of science need not undermine, and can in fact reinforce, a sense of God's power.

The poem was written in the last year of Hopkins's life to commemorate Alphonsus' recent canonisation. For once, Hopkins was writing for an audience: the poem was to be sent to Majorca for the celebrations, and so this was not the place for startling technical innovation. Like the other poems discussed in the section of this book entitled 'Last Poems', then, it is a conventional sonnet, fourteen lines of iambic pentameter with (as usual for Hopkins) the Italian rhyme-scheme. That rhyme-scheme is instantly recognisable; the only point which might cause doubt on first reading a new Hopkins poem is whether it is in sprung rhythm or standard ('alternating') rhythm. It is easier to test for standard rhythm first, by looking to see whether any lines come close to the iambic norm (remembering that many lines will depart considerably from the norm in any poem which is not intolerably dull in rhythm). Here, lines three and six should leave no doubt that this is iambic pentameter.

In any discussion of poetry, however, there is little point in the mere description of technical features as an end in itself, or in a tedious rehearsal of the definition of a sonnet. The aim, which can be achieved only after practice, is to make the connection between the objective technical facts on the one hand and the whole meaning and force of the poem on the other: it is to show how the former contribute to the latter.

Straight away we notice some striking departues from expected metre. In line nine, for example, 'Mountain' by its very nature must be pronounced as trochaic, a stress followed by an unstress. Yet metre leads us to expect an iamb at this point in the line. The result is two hard stresses ('héws móuntain') next to each other, suggesting the energy of God's creative powers. Two equallly emphatic stresses open line ten: 'Earth, all'. The word 'all', further emphasised by the pauses before and after it, thus becomes the properly emphatic climax of the list of things which God creates. With effects such as these, rhythm alone would be enough to tell us that the contents of the parenthesis is no aside but part of the essence of the meaning. In an early draft of the poem line two read as follows:

And every scar of limb, or dint of shield

The changes in the final version of this line affect diction, alliteration, and rhythm: the reader should compare the two versions in detail to discover what effects Hopkins was aiming at.

The last two lines show striking rhythmic effects of a different kind. Hopkins might have said that the single syllable 'by' hangs below the line as if it were not counted in the scansion; alternatively, we may regard it as elided into the following word 'of', so that both occupy the space of a single unstress. Again in the final line 'Majorca' elides into 'Alfonso', an elision demanded by scansion and made easy by the vowels. So, just when the words themselves describe the slow passage of time, rhythm for a moment picks up into a quicker pace as two syllables hurriedly crowd into the space reserved for one. These lines in different ways are (strange to say) both swift and slow at the same time: have we not just heard of a God who is likewise? And as rhythm ripples unexpectedly below the surface we catch a glimpse of disturbances within – the very point about Alfonso's inner life.

Notice how the poem is content to follow, rather than strain against, the shape of the sonnet (quite unlike the way that 'Thou art indeed just, Lord' achieves its effects). Each of the three sentences occupies exactly one of the major divisions of the sonnet form, as if poured into a mould. To put it another way, the units of syntax coincide exactly with the units of metre (when a sentence ends, it is also a line-end) and also with the 'closures' shaped by the recurrences of rhyme at the ends of lines four, eight, and fourteen. The poem's material rests easily within the constraints of its 'body'. It is not fanciful to see this too as being intimately connected with what is said about Alfonso. The outward circumstances of his life made a contrast with his inner struggles; Hopkins replaces that contrast with a correspondence, everything at one with itself. As I shall suggest, the poem ends with a stress on peace; but its form by itself provides an impressive image of an overarching peace.

As often in Hopkins, the poem's alliterative patterns are too complex to analyse exhaustively here. We may observe, though, that much of the alliteration is of the most noticeable and emphatic kind, in which successive words begin with the same consonant, as in 'war within', 'Veins violets', 'tall trees'. At other times the alliterative sounds are more distant from each other, as in 'while . . . went . . . world without . . . watched' in the last three lines. In either case the effect is to bind things together and give a sense of inevitability to what is said. After so many alliterative *pairs*, however, the *triplet* at 'crowd career with conquest' comes with a particular emphasis which is appropriate to the triumphant note of those words. But alliteration in good poetry is not just a decorative or emphatic device: by drawing a parallel between apparently unconnected words or phrases it can of itself create meaning. See, for instance, how alliteration combines with a parallel structure in phrasing to point up an analogy between 'more and more' (line 11) and 'years and years' (line 13). 'More and more' described God's creative ways; we therefore have to see something of his creative presence in the 'years and years' which might otherwise have seemed a barren stretch of wasted time.

Part of the poem's success is that it describes spiritual struggle in *general* terms (though we know it applies to Alfonso), and does so in the middle, not at the end: thus when the end is reached Hopkins is free to concentrate on evoking images of triumph ('conquest') and of a patient humility and devotion to duty which create the impression of peace – an impression remarkable in that is is achieved against the odds, the very opposite of the inner turmoil we have been told of. Another reason why those 'years and years' spent in a 'world without event' make their strong impression is because they are in such contrast to the images of violent action (the trumpet, the 'gashed flesh' and 'galled shield') with which the poem opened. In this way Alfonso's humble occupation of porter comes to seem almost a heavenly reward. It is as if God's patient vigilance extends to watching over the outer circumstances of Alfonso's life, providing a tranquil refuge for him just as he guards the tranquillity of those within the college. There can be no doubt that Hopkins took to heart the life-story of one whose fierce spiritual trials and humility had something in common with his own. For Alfonso, if not for himself, he could imagine an outcome of patience and peace. It is that imaginative act of faith which provides the poem's moving conclusion.

REVISION QUESTIONS

1. What do you understand by (a) inscape (b) sprung rhythm? Explain each concept using examples drawn from the poetry.

2. Other than the shipwreck itself, what do you take to be the central themes of 'The Wreck of the Deutschland'?

3. What connections and parallels can you see between Part the First and Part the Second of 'The Wreck of the Deutschland'?

4. In what ways does the poetic form of 'The Wreck of the Deutschland' contribute to its meaning?

5. Analyse in detail the relation between octave and sestet in any one of the Welsh Sonnets.

6. Illustrate from the Welsh sonnets some of Hopkins's characteristic uses of language and imagery, and explain the poetic effects which they make possible.

7. Illustrate from the poems Hopkins's conception of God's presence in nature and in man.

8. Find instances of difficulty and of simplicity in Hopkins's poetry. How successful is each?

9. Using evidence drawn from the poetry, argue for or against the view that Hopkins's treatment of human beings is less successful than his treatment of the world of nature.

10. Discuss Hopkins's attitude to work, labour, and the organisation of society as revealed in the poems.

11. In what ways may Hopkins be seen as a Romantic poet? as a Victorian? as a 'modern' poet? Give instances from the poetry.

12. 'Feeling, love in particular, is the great moving power and spring of verse.' Discuss and illustrate how far this remark of Hopkins's seems to apply to his own poetry.

FURTHER READING

Hopkins's writings

The Poems of Gerard Manley Hopkins, 4th edn, ed. W. H. Gardner and N. H. MacKenzie (Oxford University Press, 1967).
The Journals and Papers of Gerard Manley Hopkins, ed. Humphry House and Graham Storey (Oxford University Press, 1959).
The Letters of Gerard Manley Hopkins to Robert Bridges, ed. C. C. Abbott (Oxford University Press, 1935).
The Correspondence of Gerard Manley Hopkins and Richard Watson Dixon, ed. C. C. Abbott (Oxford University Press, 1935).
Further Letters of Gerard Manley Hopkins, ed. C. C. Abbott (Oxford University Press, 1938).
The Sermons and Devotional Writings of Gerard Manley Hopkins, ed. Christopher Devlin, S. J. (Oxford University Press, 1959).

Commentaries on the poems

Norman H. MacKenzie, *A Reader's Guide to Gerard Manley Hopkins* (Thames & Hudson, 1981).
Donald McChesney, *A Hopkins Commentary* (University of London Press, 1968).
Paul L. Mariani, *A Commentary on the Complete Poems of Gerard Manley Hopkins* (Cornell University Press, 1970).

Critical introductions

Graham Storey, *A Preface to Hopkins* (Longman, 1981).
R. K. R. Thornton, *G. M. Hopkins: The Poems* (Arnold, 1973).

Collections of critical essays

G. M. Hopkins: Poems. A Casebook, ed. Margaret Bottrall, (Macmillan, 1975).
Hopkins: A Collection of Critical Essays, ed. G. H. Hartman (Twentieth-Century Views) (Prentice-Hall, 1966).

Longer critical studies

W. H. Gardner, *Gerard Manley Hopkins, 1844-89: a Study of Poetic Idiosyncracy in Relation to Poetic Tradition* (2 vols), revised edition (Oxford University Press, 1966).
Elisabeth W. Schneider, *The Dragon in the Gate: Studies in the Poetry of G. M. Hopkins* (University of California Press, 1968).